# An Unexpected Cookbook

## The Unofficial Book of Hobbit Cookery

Chris-Rachael Oseland

## Dedication

To Anne, the best person I've ever known.
Here's to the next 20 years of friendship.

## Acknowledgements and Thanks

This book would not be possible without the literary classics that are *The Hobbit* and *The Lord of the Rings* trilogy. If you've only seen the movies, you are in for an epic delight when you read the books. Many posthumous thanks to J.R.R. Tolkien for creating the fantasy genre as we know it today.

# Table of Contents

# Introduction: The Shire Pantry

In Tolkien's letters, he makes it clear the Shire was based on a very specific time and place - namely, the English village where he spent much of his childhood in the 1890's. I've done my best to adapt authentic period recipes to fit the very specific limitations Tolkien placed on the Shire. Honestly, it's a fun challenge. The end result is hearty comfort food inspired as loyally as possible by *The Hobbit*.

Country food in the 1890's bore little resemblance to the city food we associate with wealthy Victorians. While the wealthy would enjoy internationally inspired dishes like Kedgeree for breakfast (a milky fish stir fry made from rice and a tragic, third-hand misunderstanding of curry) their country cousins had to make do with old fashioned staples like bacon, eggs, and toast. For every shudder inducing horror you've read about Victorian city cooking, there's an equally familiar old-fashioned farm dish that's still with us today. That country cooking stuck around because it was delicious.

The Shire represented everything Tolkien loved about English country life. After losing all but one of his friends in World War I then living through the horrors of World War II, it's no surprise he wanted to celebrate and venerate a gentler way of life he saw rapidly disappearing as the world around him grew smaller and bleaker. Instead of technologies to bring people together, Tolkien saw the expansion of trains and later cars as ways for the grimy industrial world to impose itself on peaceful country life.

To keep the Shire wholesomely isolated in time and memory, he actively excluded all new world foods except tobacco, coffee, and potatoes, all of which he thoroughly enjoyed.

That means no vanilla in baked goods, no chocolate in desserts, and no pineapple (which the Victorians adored). On the savory side, that meant no tomatoes, which were well loved by Victorians, no squash, maize (sweet corn), or common beans, all of which had all become quite entrenched in the everyday English cooking of his day.

In addition to excluding new world crops, he also limited influences from further west to what the Crusaders brought back with them. There are plenty of references to food made with the popular imported medieval staple spices of cinnamon, ginger, nutmeg, allspice, and cloves as well as expensive fruits such as lemons and oranges. But that was where he drew the line. There is no rice in the Shire, much less a nice plate of curry. Instead, the Shire exists in an idealized, purely English world untouched by wars or Empires.

Out of respect for both the source recipes and the village life, Tolkien's Shire evokes, you'll find quite a few recipes include ways to use the leftovers for future meals. During the 1890's, when Tolkien was a boy, food cost up to ⅔ of a middle-class family's income. The people he based the Shire on would've squeezed every last drop of flavor and use from any scrap of food that came into their possession. There's a creativity applied to repurposing leftovers that are mostly forgotten today.

You can feel the love and nostalgia for that hearty country cuisine every time the Hobbits eat. The end result of all that thrifty cleverness is often insanely more delicious than anything you can buy pre-made at your local grocer.

That means hearty Hobbit home cooking is limited to these traditional English staples:

## VEGETABLES

Potatoes* (his one new world exception)
Carrots
Turnips
Beets
Onions
Garlic
Shallots
Asparagus
Green Beans
Salad Greens
Cucumbers
Lettuces
Radishes
Cabbages

## GRAINS

Wheat
Oats
Barley

## FRUITS

Apples
Pears
Plums
Apricots
Raisins
Quince
Currants

## MEATS

Mutton or Lamb
Pork
Chicken
Beef
Rabbit
Venison
Fish

## HERBS

Rosemary
Thyme
Parsley
Basil
Dill
Sage
Tarragon
Chervil
Chives
Savory

## FATS:

Butter
Bacon Grease
Lard
Suet

In addition, country folk and Hobbits alike would've enjoyed epic quantities of fresh butter and white flour in every meal. The Shire is a land of delicious cakes, pies, and bread, all made from things your great-grandmother would've considered good, healthy food.

Inside these pages, you'll find one chapter for each traditional Hobbit meal. In addition to being based on historical recipes revised to fit Tolkien's specific limitations on the Shire, the dishes have the following themes.

- **Breakfast** - hot, fast, traditional morning food
- **Second Breakfast** - cold, sturdy pies full of meat, veg and fruit to fuel a small adventure
- **Elevenses** - a hearty selection of bread to tide you over until Luncheon
- **Luncheon** - lighter fare appropriate for a pub setting
- **Afternoon Tea** - sweet biscuits, cakes, and buns to accompany a caffeinated pick-me-up
- **Supper** - a hot meal of meat, veg, and mushrooms with a sweet finish
- **Dinner** - slow cooked roasts and puddings that take hours to make, but are well worth the wait

Whether you want to make an epic dinner fit for a king or bring a little period flair to a geeky gathering, you'll find something in these pages for every Tolkien fan.

# Breakfast

In Tolkien's day, ovens were slow to heat and expensive to keep fired up. If you wanted a hot breakfast, you could either get up at 4 am to start stoking the flames or make a simpler dish in a pot or skillet. Even wealthy or upper class families woke to foods like Kedgeree (fish and rice stir fry), poached fruit, and cold cuts of meat left over from the previous night's supper. Even faster and easier options like fried eggs, sausages, and toasted bread were looked down on as fast, cheap, country fare fit only for farm workers.

In keeping with the rustic, egalitarian spirit of the Shire, all these breakfast recipes are (relatively, for the time) fast, affordable dishes you could make in a skillet while waiting for the coffee to brew. Food used to consume up to ⅔ of a family's budget, so a lot of these historic recipes also include economical ways to repurpose leftovers or stretch out expensive ingredients.

# Mushroom and Bacon Hash

Hash is quite possibly the best excuse for not taking a second helping of potatoes at dinner. As leftovers, they take on a whole new, wonderful form the next morning.

A nice plate of hash may seem a slow dish for an indulgent weekend morning, but back in Tolkien's day, it was the equivalent of fast food. It may not seem like it to us, but compared to an upper-class English breakfast, hash could be whipped up in little time using whatever leftovers you had on hand. Since Hobbits are known to have mushrooms at every meal, throwing a couple handfuls in a pan would add great flavor to this quick morning dish.

You can use whatever savory ingredients you have around. Substitute homemade sausage for the bacon. Delude yourself into pretending you're having a healthy breakfast by tossing in a handful of cubed, roasted cauliflower. Sweeten the dish by chopping up a cooked carrot from last night's roast. The key is making sure everything you throw in is already fully cooked and cut into pieces about the same size.

*8 slices bacon*
*3 c / 300 g leftover baked potatoes cut into cubes\**
*2 c / 150 g mushrooms, diced*
*1 onion, diced*
*1 garlic clove, chopped*
*2 tsp coarse salt*
*½ tsp fresh ground black pepper*
*1 tsp kitchen herbs (optional)*

Fry your bacon in a cast iron skillet. If you know you can't resist fresh, hot, bacon, add in a couple extra strips to munch on while the hash is cooking.

While the bacon crisps up, peel any leftover baked or roasted potatoes from last night and cut them into rough cubes. Don't use mashed potatoes. You need a little more solidity than that. In a pinch, you can always chop up leftover Boxty (pg. 123) or Pan Fried Tater Cakes (pg. 68). The point is to use up your leftovers while making a hot breakfast. Once you're done contemplating last night's potatoes, peel and dice the onion.

Dice up a cup of whatever leftover mushrooms you have from last night. The flavor of the spices or sauce they were cooked in will add to the hash. If neither dinner nor supper left you with any leftover mushrooms, go ahead and dice up some fresh ones. You'll want to finish the dish with some kitchen herbs (thyme and basil work particularly well) to bump up the flavor.

Remove the bacon. You should now have a pan of delicious grease. Turn the heat down to medium. Add your diced onion and stir well. Let it cook for 2-3 minutes or until it turns translucent.

Now add the diced potatoes, salt, and pepper. Give it all a good stir, so it plays nicely together and let it cook for a couple minutes while you crumble up the bacon. Once the bacon is in pieces, fold the salty crumbles and your mushrooms into the potato and onion mix until you have a beautiful, aromatic mess. Press down hard on the mixture to flatten it out. This will result in a crunchy bottom crust with tender potatoes on top.

Now here is the hard part - walk away for a couple minutes. Don't fuss with it or check it or stir it. Just let your hash sizzle away over medium heat for about 10 minutes. When you come back, it should be beautifully browned on the bottom and warmed all the way through to the top.

If you used enough bacon grease, the hash should slide right out of the skillet in one piece and onto a waiting plate. If you have some seasoned mushrooms leftover from last night, sprinkle them on top now. If not, sprinkle your fresh hash with 1 tsp of your favorite kitchen herbs (thyme, basil, or rosemary) along with a pinch of coarse salt to bring out the flavors.

To keep yourself from burning your mouth on the deliciousness of fresh hash, fry up a batch of eggs in the last of the bacon grease while the hash itself cools enough to eat.

**VEGAN VARIATION**

Instead of bacon, heat 4 tbsp of olive oil over medium heat in a large skillet. Cook the chopped onion for 2-3 minutes, or until it turns translucent. Add 1 cup of vegan crumbles from your grocer's freezer section and cook until the meat substitute is warmed through. Go ahead and add in your potatoes and mushrooms, give it all a good stir, and press down hard to flatten it out. Let it cook undisturbed for 10 minutes or until it's crispy and brown on bottom.

This isn't a good dish for substituting seitan or tofu as they're both prone to falling apart in the pan from all the stirring and squishing. However, it's a great dish for any leftover cooked vegetables from last night's dinner. Just make sure they're cut the same size as the potatoes and are included in a ratio of no more than 1 part random veggies for every 3 parts potato.

# Stewed Apples and Prunes

This pruney dish would've been a favorite of grandparents and curmudgeons of any age when Tolkien was a boy. The Victorians adored their cheap sugar, but their grandparents would've still had a palate for the more naturally sweet dishes of their youth. This old- fashioned dish is based on medieval recipes combining the natural sweetness of apples with the natural sweetness of prunes plus a bit of wine or alcoholic apple juice. People with a strong sweet tooth could add a tablespoon of honey. The sweet taste, soft texture, and high fiber made it a go-to dish for anyone endowed with more wisdom than teeth.

*1 c / 250 ml sweet white wine or hard apple cider*
*10 dried pitted prunes*
*4 whole cloves*
*1 inch /2.5 cm piece cinnamon stick*
*3 tart green apples*
*½ tsp salt*
*1 tbsp honey (optional)*

Add your wine or cider, cloves, cinnamon stick, and salt to a medium pot and bring them to a boil.

While you're waiting for your pot to boil, quarter the apples and cut out the cores. No need to skin them. They add a nice bit of texture.

Once the liquid is boiling, add the apple skin side down. Top them with the prunes. Turn the heat down to low and simmer for 15-20 minutes, or until the apples are tender and the liquid is mostly absorbed. If you'd like, you can stir in an extra tbsp of honey before serving.

Stewed apples and prunes weren't just limited to breakfast. Sure, they make a fantastic oatmeal porridge topping, but they're equally good served over freshly toasted day old bread. Historically, breakfast leftovers might have also shown up at dinner with a bit of cream as a dessert.

Serving meats and sweets together has gone out of fashion, but they were an incredibly popular combination from Medieval through Victorian times. If you want another way to experience a taste of the era, this recipe makes a fantastic tasting yet stealthily healthy topping for baked pork chops or bone-in chicken thighs.

If you use it as a meat topping, increase the liquid by ¼ c if baking in a covered dish or ½ c if baking uncovered. Once your pork chops or chicken thighs are completely cooked, remove the meat and collect all the extra liquid from the bottom of the pan. Mix in 1 tsp of coarse salt. You now have an excellent sauce for the grains or carbs of your choice. Cooked barley would be well loved by Hobbits, but visitors to the Shire could toss the fruity liquid in their rice, couscous, quinoa, or mixed grain blend (all of which would've been quite novel to Hobbits). This makes a sweet and easy complimentary side dish. If your modern family finds it too repetitive to have their meat and carb coated in the same sauce, you can store the liquid in the fridge for a few days. Reheat it to add a little quick and easy flavor to grains, carrots, or green vegetables.

# Morning Oat Porridge

Since you have all those tasty stewed apples and prunes sitting around, why not make some hearty porridge to go with them? Porridge was a generic term for any boiled grains made soft enough you could eat them with a spoon. Since it was mostly a breakfast staple eaten while half asleep, people used whatever grains were cheapest. In Tolkien's day, that usually meant oats in the north or wheat in the south, though semolina, bulgur, or barley weren't uncommon.

While it wasn't a taste sensation, porridge was known to be pretty forgiving. It was easy to reheat if you didn't have time for a new batch, easy to thin out if you had unexpected guests, and easy to dress up with other flavors when you needed a little morning excitement.

**Porridge:**
*1 tbsp butter*
*1 c /100 g porridge oats*
*3 c / 710 ml boiling water*
*3/4 c /180 ml whole milk + extra for serving*
*½ tsp coarse salt*

**Topping:**
*1 tbsp brown sugar*
*1/2 tsp cinnamon*
*2 tbsp chopped raisins, sultanas, or dates (optional)*

The key to really tasty porridge is toasting the grains first. If you've only had oatmeal from a packet, prepare to be shocked by the difference.

Melt your butter in a large saucepan over medium-high heat. Pour in the oats and give them a good stir until they're completely coated in butter. Keep stirring continuously for the next two minutes. You want to get all the oats nice and toasty without burning any.

Once the oats are toasted, drown them in boiling water, add your salt, and give them a good hearty stir. Turn the heat down to medium low. Put a lid on the pot and let them simmer for 25 minutes. Resist the urge to fuss with them. Oats really are this easy.

Come back 25 minutes later and pour in the milk. Gently stir the milk into the porridge. Keep cooking for another 10-12 minutes, or until the porridge reaches your desired thickness.

Ladle the hot porridge into bowls. You can top it with leftover cooked fruit (such as the stewed apples and prunes or leftover roast apples from last night's dinner) or just add some brown sugar, cinnamon, and whatever dried fruit you have around the house.

# Frumenty Wheat Porridge

While oats were the grain of choice in the north, people in the south preferred wheat. Since The Shire was based on a village square in the middle of the country, Hobbits would no doubt get to enjoy both.

On a day to day basis, most people in the south would've eaten the same style of porridge as northerners, substituting wheat in the place of oats. Only the wealthy could regularly afford to add expensive yet tasty ingredients like saffron and pine nuts. That meant for working class households; frumenty was usually only served around Christmas as a special holiday treat.

**Porridge:**
*1 tbsp butter*
*1 c / 200 g bulgur wheat*
*1 c / 220 ml whole milk*
*2 c / 470 ml water*
*⅓ c / 100 ml whole cream*
*⅓ c / 50 g dried cherries*
*⅓ c / 50 g currants (or raisins)*
*2 egg yolks, beaten*
*4 saffron strands*
*⅓ c / 50 g brown sugar*

**Topping:**
*½ tbsp butter*
*1 tbsp pine nuts*
*⅔ c 100 g flaked almonds*
*⅓ c 100 ml whole cream*

Just like regular porridge, frumenty's rich flavor gains, even more, depth when you toast the grains. Melt your butter in a large saucepan over medium-high heat. Add the wheat and constantly stir for about two minutes, or until all the grains are toasted. Turn the heat down to medium and add the water. Give that a good stir, then add the whole milk. If you add the milk first, you risk scalding it.

Unlike the oats, which you could abandon for nearly half an hour, wheat needs constant attention. Keep stirring while you bring the pot to a gentle boil. Once it starts boiling, continue stirring regularly for 8-10 minutes, or until most of the liquid is absorbed and the wheat is tender. If your pot runs dry before the wheat has softened up, add another ¼ c / 60 ml of water and keep stirring it for another 5-6 minutes. Mix in the cherries and currants, then cover the pan and take it off the heat for 10 minutes so the wheat can cool.

When you come back, mix in the heavy cream. You need to let the wheat cool before mixing in the cream or else you risk the dairy curdling. Now put the pot back over a medium heat and slowly bring it back to a gentle boil. Stir frequently to keep anything from burning. Once the mix is boiling again, carefully stir in the beaten egg yolks. When they're well mixed, add the saffron strands and brown sugar. Keep mixing everything for another 1-2 minutes, so the brown sugar melts into the porridge, and the saffron strands have a chance to come in contact with as much of the grain as possible.

Remove the pan from the heat, cover it with a lid, and let it sit for 5-10 minutes for the flavors to mingle. While you wait, prepare the topping. Melt ½ tsp butter in a skillet over medium-high heat. Add the pine nuts and flaked almonds. Stir constantly for 1-2 minutes while the nuts toast. Be warned, if you look away for a second, pine nuts will instantly go from pale and chewy to burnt. Keep a close eye on them during the toasting.

To serve, fill bowls with frumenty, pour in a splash of cream, and top each one with a tbsp or two of freshly toasted nuts. If the expense and fuss of pine nuts are outside your budget, you can simply top the rich porridge with a splash of cream and plenty of dried cherries and currants.

# Stuffed Poached Pears

If you find yourself entertaining unexpected guests, this rustic, seasonal breakfast is a quick, easy way to make a simple breakfast of leftovers seem fit for a brunch with the king of the dwarves.

*4 large firm pears*
*2 c / 470 ml apple cider, pear cider, or white wine*
*¼ c / 50 g sugar*
*1 tsp cinnamon*
*2 c / 450 g leftover oat porridge or frumenty*
*1 c / 220 g leftover Stewed Apples and Prunes (pg. 14) from Breakfast or leftover Roasted Apples (pg. 131) from Supper, chopped*
*4 tbsp heavy cream*

This is honestly a lot easier than it looks. It's mostly a matter of heating up leftovers while a pot simmers. You can do it half brain dead while waiting for coffee to brew.

Pour the cider or wine in a wide stew pot. Add the sugar and cinnamon and bring it to a boil over medium-high heat.

While you're waiting for the booze to boil, peel the pears. Cut them in half lengthwise and scoop out the seeds and a little interior flesh. These are about to become edible bowls, so get rid of anything you don't want to eat while still keeping the pear's shape.

Add the pears cut side down to the pot of bubbling booze. Put a lid on it and turn the heat down to medium low. Let the pears gently simmer for about 10-12 minutes. Open the pot, carefully flip the pears over, then put the lid back on and continue simmering for another 10-12 minutes, or until the pears are tender but not mushy.

While the pears are simmering away, splash a little milk in yesterday's porridge or frumenty to loosen it up. Once it reaches the right consistency, warm it through. You can use another pot, or if you don't mind modern magic, just toss it in the microwave for a minute or two. Do the same thing with some leftover baked apples from last night's dessert or stewed apples and prunes from yesterday's breakfast.

Use a slotted spoon to lift the pears onto a serving platter carefully. Remember, from this point on; your main goal is presentation. Arrange the pear halves cut-side up on a platter. Spoon the furmenty or porridge in the middle. Make a little well and top that with some leftover apples or dried fruit. Finish them off by splashing a tbsp of heavy cream over each assembled pear half.

Make sure everyone else finishes their first cup of coffee or tea while your pears cook. You want them to be awake and properly impressed when you bring this to the table.

# Apple and Cherry Griddle Cakes

Bread is delicious, but it takes forever. Every culture with wheat has come up with some type of fast and easy flat breads, and Victorian England was no exception.

These quick, easy morning griddle cakes are the ancestor of modern American pancakes. As a new world food, maple syrup would be totally unknown in the Shire. People in Tolkien's day preferred their morning griddle cakes to be naturally sweetened with plenty of seasonal, local fruit and topped with a sprinkle of extra sugar and cinnamon.

*1 large tart apple, peeled and shredded*
*1/4 c / 60 g butter, melted + more for frying*
*2 eggs*
*1 c / 220 ml whole milk*
*1 1/2 c / 190 g flour*
*1 1/4 tsp baking powder*
*1/4 tsp ground cinnamon*
*2 tbsp white sugar*
*½ tsp salt*
*⅓ c / 50 g dried cherries*

Start by peeling and shredding your apple until it could be mistaken for raw hash browns. Mix the shredded apple with the butter, eggs, and milk.

In another bowl, whisk together your flour, baking powder, cinnamon, sugar, and salt.

Once your dry goods are blended, add them to the apple mix. Throw in the cherries while you're at it. Mix everything together until it just combines into a batter. No need to over mix it.

If you're making bacon or sausage for breakfast, fry that up before starting your pancakes. That way you can cook the cakes in delicious meat grease. If not, feel free to just use butter.

Lower heat and longer cooking times are the keys to making lovely golden brown griddle cakes that flip easily with no mess. The faster and hotter you cook them, the more likely they are to wind up burned at the edges and raw in the middle. Cook these over medium heat - no hotter.

You now have a choice to make. You can either pour in three to four small griddle cakes using no more than ¼ c of batter at a time, or you can be bold and daring and pour a single large cake into the middle of the skillet using ½ c of batter. The smaller cakes are good for large crowds while the bigger ones are a faster way to get a family breakfast to the table.

If your skillet isn't already pre-greased from sausage or bacon, generously smear it with butter before adding the batter. Instead of watching the time, watch the griddle cakes. When the edges start to lift up from the pan and bubbles rise to the surface of the middle, they're ready to flip. Any sooner than that and you'll wind up with a wet, sloppy mess stretched across your pan.

After flipping, brown your small griddle cakes for another 1-2 minutes or the large ones for 3-4 minutes to finish them.

Sprinkle the hot cakes with extra sugar and cinnamon or spread them with fresh raspberry jam. If you have extras, store them in the fridge overnight then reheat in a 350F / 180C oven for 5-6 minutes.

**VEGAN VARIATION**

Substitute almond milk for the whole milk. The flavor nicely compliments the shredded apples. To make up for the flavor imparted by animal fats, increase the sugar by 1 tbsp, increase the cinnamon by ¼ tbsp, and add a generous pinch of salt to the batter. Substitute a neutral flavored cooking oil for the butter in the batter, then make sure to wipe some more cooking oil across the skillet between each batch of griddle cakes.

# Home Made Country Sausage Patties

Unlike proper sausages, which were a great way to preserve meat before refrigeration, country sausage was a way to make good use of odd scraps and fatty bits, odd cuts, and leftover meat. All you needed to do was change the texture and add some aromatic herbs to cover any lingering smell.

The key to getting the texture that separates hamburger patties from breakfast sausage is to run the meat through the finest grain of a meat grinder. Don't be afraid to ask your butcher to put ground meat from the case through a second, finer grind.

*2 1/4 lbs / 1 kg finely ground, somewhat fatty pork (or a mix of pork, beef, or the meat of your choice)*
*2 garlic cloves, minced*
*2 tsp fresh sage leaves*
*2 tsp fresh thyme leaves*
*½ tsp fresh rosemary leaves*
*1 tsp fennel seeds*
*½ tsp nutmeg*
*½ tsp cloves*
*1 ½ tbsp dark brown sugar*

This couldn't be easier. First, mix everything but the meat into a spicy paste. Then spread the paste over the surface of the meat, coating as much of it as possible. Finally, knead the spices into the meat. Really dig your fingers in there. You want to integrate the spices as thoroughly as possible.

Pack the spice infused meat into a tidy ball, cover it, and let it rest in your fridge for up to an hour, preferably for at least six. Honestly, the best way to make this is to mix your meat and spices before bed. Let them rest overnight, and they'll be ready for you to cook first thing in the morning when you're still brain dead and waiting for your first cup of tea.

Heat a skillet to medium-high. Rip off golf ball sized wedges of meat and squish them into discs. Let the meat cook for about five minutes on each side, or until browned on the exterior and completely cooked through the middle.

If you used a good, fatty meat, you'd now have some delicious grease in your skillet, just waiting for you to crack in an egg or fry some potatoes. If you used lean meats, you might need to smear a little butter in the skillet to keep the sausage from sticking during the cooking process.

Country sausage patties are best hot and fresh, but they'll stay good in the fridge for at least two days or in the freezer for up to 3 months. Reheat them in a warm buttered skillet or crumble them up to use in other recipes.

# Mushroom Omelet

Oversized modern omelets are seen as a decadent breakfast for one, but historically, they were often thrown together when you had more mouths to feed than you had fresh eggs. Add a little milk and last night's veggies, and suddenly three eggs can be turned into a hearty breakfast for four.

Fresh ingredients are great, but if you want to stay true to the rustic village that inspired the Shire, you can never be afraid of leftovers. If you have any mushrooms or onions leftover from last night's supper, act like a Hobbit and by using them in the place of fresh vegetables. It'll save you time and add extra flavor. Instead of bacon, you can always use a scant handful of the last bits of meat plucked off a chicken or a wedge of roast too small for a sandwich. A good English country omelet was an exercise in creatively stretching a few ingredients into a hearty breakfast that could feed a small army. Timing and technique are more important than exact ingredients.

*1 tbsp butter*
*¼ onion, sliced thin*
*1/2 c /75 g button mushrooms, sliced*
*1 clove garlic, crushed*
*1 tsp fresh minced garden herbs (thyme, basil, marjoram, or a mix)*
*1 tsp salt, divided*
*3 large eggs*
*3 tbsp milk*
*3 slices crispy bacon (optional)*
*3 tbsp shredded gruyere (or your favorite cheese)*

The key to a good omelet is temperature control and patience. You need to let the eggs cook slowly. Otherwise, the bottom will burn while the middle stays an inedible liquid. If you stick with a medium heat and don't fuss with it, you'll master this easy breakfast dish in no time.

If you're adding bacon, start by frying up five strips in a large skillet over medium high heat. Three go in the omelet; two go in your mouth. If you're a master of self-control around fresh, crispy bacon, you can just fry the three.

Remove the bacon from the skillet and replace it with butter. Once the butter has melted into the bacon fat, turn the heat down to medium and gently fry the onions, mushrooms, and garlic for 3-4 minutes, or until the mushrooms turn translucent and the garlic barely starts to brown.

While the onion mix cooks, whisk together your eggs, milk, and ½ tsp salt. The more air you can get into the eggs the better.

After the onion mix has spent 3-4 minutes in the skillet, add the kitchen herbs and remaining ½ tsp of salt. Stir the mix continuously for the next minute, so the herbs get a chance to coat everything without burning. After a minute, slide the veggies onto a waiting plate.

Now it's time for your eggs. Turn the heat down to medium. If your skillet feels too warm, take it off the heat for a minute or two to cool down.

Pour in your well-whisked egg blend. Now here's the hardest part. Walk away. Just leave it alone for 3-4 minutes while the bottom of the eggs firms up. This isn't scrambled eggs. You don't need to make curds. Just let the whisked eggs and heat work their magic. You can start interacting with it again when the edges are cooked through and start to release slightly from the sides. At this point, the middle will still be a little runny.

Crumble up however much bacon you have left and sprinkle it over ½ of the omelet. Top that with your sautéed veggies. Sprinkle the cheese on top and watch as it starts its transformation into the glue that binds all great foods together.

Using a very wide spatula (or two smaller ones and a lot of dexterity), fold the naked side of the omelet over the filled side. If you did it neatly, congratulations! If it ripped, don't stress. The ripped side is now the bottom. No one needs to know.

Carefully slide your omelet out of the pan and onto a waiting plate. You used both butter and bacon grease the omelet shouldn't have any problems easing out of the pan. If you ripped it, place another plate on top and flip it over.  The rip is hidden from sight, and you now have one beautiful presentation omelet.

You can cut the omelet into quarters as a hearty standalone breakfast. If you have unexpected guests, cut it into smaller slices as the main breakfast course served alongside some freshly fried potatoes and a couple leftover buns from last night.

# Second Breakfast

Second Breakfast is the perfect time for adventuring.

All of these dishes can be made the night before and carried in your rucksack as you sneak over the hedgerows and out into the world beyond the Shire.

To ensure your food doesn't get crushed or fall to pieces in your rucksack, our Second Breakfast includes a full meal in the form of durable hand pies. You have a pork pie for your meat, mushroom pie for your veg, and apple pie for your fruit with a nice hearty slice of porter cake for dessert.  If you have space in your bag, Hobbits are known to flesh out their second breakfast with cold roast chicken, hard boiled eggs plus some pickles and mustard for flavor.

You can easily make all three pies at once using the same handy short crust pastry dough.

# Short Crust Pastry Dough

*2 ½ c / 240 g flour*
*⅓ c / 80 ml cold water*
*½ c / 250 g room temperature butter*
*2 tbsp sugar*
*1 tsp salt*
*1 egg for optional egg wash*

A hearty short crust pastry is one of the best options for adventurers. The small pies hold up well no matter how many supplies you cram in your pack. That density means you only need a few to fill up. Plus, they're just plain delicious.

To make the pastry, start by whisking together the flour, sugar, and salt. Next, add in the room temperature butter. Yes, room temperature. Cold butter makes for a flaky crust, but there were no refrigerators in the Shire. Furthermore, while flaky crusts are delicious, pastries made from them would shed all over your pack. If you want a solid hand pie that can stand up to some abuse without emptying its contents all over your pack, stick with a solid foundation of room temperature butter.

Work the butter into the flour using your fingers until it magically transforms from a greasy lump into a coarse, gravelly meal. Gradually moisten the crumbles with cold water. Use just enough to bind the meal together into a pastry dough. You don't want it getting too wet and sticky. Knead the dough a few times then pack it into a disc. Store the disc in the fridge until you're ready to use it.

**VEGAN VARIATION**

Substitute room temperature coconut oil for the butter and add an extra tsp of salt and tablespoon of sugar to make up for losing the flavor of the butter.

# Mushroom, Beef & Onion Hand Pies

Its well-known Hobbits love mushrooms. These hearty hand pies are an inexpensive and durable way to bring the best taste of the Shire along on any adventure. Enjoy a couple for a quick Elevenses or save them for supper when the crust can soak up a little mutton gravy.

While Hobbits are well known for enjoying meat as much as they do mushrooms, it's easy enough to make this vegan in case you're serving visitors on their own adventure from distant lands.

*1 tbsp butter, bacon grease, or cooking oil*
*1 large yellow onion, diced*
*1 pint / 450 g mushrooms, minced*
*6 garlic cloves, minced*
*1 1/2 tsp salt*
*1 tsp ground black pepper*
*3 1/2 tsp paprika*
*1/3 tsp fennel seed*
*1 tsp savory (or rubbed sage)*
*1 tsp rosemary*
*1 lb. / 450 g ground beef, pork, mutton or a mix (or vegan crumbles)*
*1 batch short crust pastry dough*

To make the filling, melt your fat of choice in a large skillet over medium-high heat. Add the diced onions and let them cook for about 5 minutes. You want to sweat out a lot of the moisture. Add the mushrooms and garlic, then cook them for another 3-4 minutes, stirring often.

Toss in the salt, pepper, paprika, fennel, savory, and rosemary. Give it all a good hearty stir and cook for another 2 minutes.

If you're making vegan pies, you can either stop now for an all-vegetable filling or add a pound of frozen vegan crumbles and another tbsp of cooking oil. The crumbles are fully cooked, so you're literally just warming them though and mixing them with the spices.

If you're making the meaty version, slide the mushroom mix out of the pan and let it patiently wait its turn in a nearby bowl. Replace it with the ground meat, which you should cook until browned through.

You may want to drain the fat but don't. That precious fluid not only helps bind your ingredients together but also helps preserve the food.

Dump the cooked mushroom mix back in the pan and give it a good stir until everything is well blended. Now turn off the heat and let the filling cool slightly. If you don't already have a disc of dough in the fridge, this is a good time to make the crust.

## ASSEMBLY

Lightly flour your work surface. Break off about ¼ of the short crust pastry dough and roll it out until it's no less than a ¼-⅛ inch / 3-6 mm thick. You really don't want it any thinner. Remember, these aren't delicate aristocratic nibbles. These are hearty hand pies meant to survive two days in your knapsack. Give them some backbone.

Use a four inch / 10 cm wide cookie cutter to cut out dough discs. Circles, hexes, or whatever shape you'd like are perfectly fine, so long as you are confident you can seal it closed.

Densely pack about 2 tbsp of filling in the middle of your bottom crust. Go ahead and use your hands. It's easier. Tightly stretch a second crust on top of it. Use the edge of a fork to crimp the crusts closed. (Or be fancy with your favorite technique. Have fun with it.) Make sure to punch a couple holes in the top for steam to escape.

Arrange your hand pies 1-2 inches / 2.5 -5 cm apart on a well-greased cookie sheet.

If you're not making vegan pies, whisk 1 egg plus 1 tbsp of water together. Use a pastry brush to paint the tops of your hand pies. If you are using the vegan option, paint the top of the crusts with a thin layer of very cold water or a dab of melted coconut oil to give them a little sheen.

Either way, bake them at 375F / 190C for 20-25 minutes, or until golden brown. Try not to eat the entire batch fresh from the oven. You need to save at least a few for adventuring.

# Pork Hand Pie

There are dozens of different techniques for making pork pies. They range from an involved, two-day long process rife with opportunities to injure yourself with hot, liquid fat to this fairly simple hand pie recipe for people who want to make up three batches of different pies in a single afternoon. Sitting down to a pork pie, mushroom pie, and apple pie makes for a balanced meal and civilized Elevenses.

Most recipes from this time period offer frustratingly vague directions like, "mix in enough flour" or "use a good quantity of pork" and tell you to mix them with, "all the right herbs."  In the spirit of the rural Victorians, feel free to start with these instructions then improvise madly.

*1 lb / 450 g pork sausage, mushed into crumbles*
*1 onion, diced*
*2 tbsp flour*
*½ tbsp thyme*
*½ tsp allspice*
*¼ tsp fresh ground black pepper*
*Pinch freshly ground nutmeg*
*Pinch coarse salt*
*1 batch short crust pastry*

You don't want hearty sausage links here. Get loose, ground country sausage (you can find it in the butcher section of larger groceries) or use your own homemade Country Sausage (pg. 24) from Breakfast. You want a loose grind full of delicious fat to bind the filling together.

Brown the sausage and remove it from the skillet. Add the onion to all that tasty grease. Cook it until the onion has sweat out most of its moisture (this helps the pies keep from getting too mushy) and started to turn a nice brown at the edges.

Once your onions are browned, turn the heat down to medium. Return the sausage to the pan and add in the thyme, allspice, nutmeg, salt, and pepper. Mix well, so everything is coated, and keep cooking for another 1-2 minutes. Now sprinkle the flour over the top of the mixture. Patiently let it soak in for about a minute before you start stirring. This should thicken up the filling and help bind it together.  Take the filling off the heat and let it cool to room temperature before stuffing your pies.

Just as with the mushroom hand pies, you want to roll your short crust pastry dough out until it's no less than ¼ - ⅛ inch / 3-6 mm thick. Use a 4 inch / 10 cm wide cookie cutter to cut it into large rounds. If you're making a big batch of different pies and don't want the first bite of every one to be a surprise, have fun using different shaped cookie cutters for each filling.

Whatever shape you use, tightly pack 2 tbsp of filling into the middle of your crust. Fold the crust over, pinch it tight, and crimp the edges tightly closed. Once the edges are crimped, punch a couple holes in the top for steam to escape.  Arrange your hand pies 1-2 inches / 2.5-5 cm apart on a well-greased cookie sheet.

Whisk 1 egg plus 1 tbsp of water together. Use a pastry brush to paint the tops of your hand pies. Once they're shiny and beautiful, bake them at 375F / 190C for 20-25 minutes, or until golden brown.

# Apple Hand Pies Two Ways

These petite apple pies are good for more than Second Breakfast. If you make enough for leftovers, they can be enjoyed either as a hearty vegetarian breakfast or as a durable tea time treat capable of keeping their shape after bumping around in your pack for a few days.

**Filling:**
*8 large, tart apples, peeled, cored and diced small*
*1 c / 200 g sugar*
*2 tsp cinnamon*
*1 tsp ginger*
*½ tsp nutmeg*
*Pinch ground cloves*
*3 tbsp butter, melted*
*2 tbsp honey*

**Crust:**
*1 batch short crust pastry plus optional additions:*
*1 tbsp sugar*
*1 tsp cinnamon*
*Extra sugar to dust the surface of the pies*

Peel and core the tart green apples of your choice. Cut the apples into a small dice. The smaller you dice them, the more filling you can pack into each pie, so don't be shy with the knife.

Mix the sugar, cinnamon, ginger, nutmeg, and a pinch of cloves in a large mixing bowl. Once they're all playing nicely together, dump the apples on top. Toss them in the spice mix until every piece of apple is coated. Now drizzle the melted butter and honey on top. Toss the apples a few more times to get the tasty fat and liquid sugar on as many pieces as possible.

Let the apple flavors mingle while you make the crust.

You can just mix up one large batch of short crust pastry and stuff ⅓ with mushroom filling, ⅓ with pork pie filling, and ⅓ with apple filling. However, if you're only making the apple pies, go ahead and sweeten the crust a little. Add 1 tbsp sugar and 1 tsp cinnamon to the flour. Once all the dry ingredients are mixed together, add the butter and water just like in the original recipe. This gives the apple pies a hint of sweetness and a nice added aroma, but it's not strictly necessary.

Once your filling and crust are ready, preheat your oven to 375F / 190C.

You can now make your pies in two shapes. Either way, start by sprinkling flour on a clean surface and rolling the dough out to ¼ inch / 3 mm thickness. Don't go much thinner or they'll be prone to falling apart after one bite.

To make a large, cupcake sized hand pies, start by generously greasing a muffin tin with butter. Remember, this isn't health food. You want the pies to slide right out with ease while also gaining a little extra crispy flavor.

Use a cookie cutter about 2 inches / 5 cm bigger around than your muffin pan wells. Press the large round piece into a well. Make sure a little bit hangs over the top.

Poke a couple vent holes in the bottom then spoon apple filling up to the top of your muffin wells.

Cut out a second circle of dough just a smidge narrower than the top of your muffin wells. Lay it on top of the filling. Pinch the overhanging filling around the top crust. You've now successfully enclosed your pies.

Poke a few vent holes in the top of the crust. Feel free to sprinkle it with a little extra cinnamon and sugar to give it a nice crunch.

Bake the cupcake sized hand pies at 375F / 190C for 45-50 min or until golden brown.

If you prefer the bite sized tea time pies, simply cut out a flat disc of dough with a 2 inch / 5 cm cutter. Pile a heaping tbsp of filling in the middle, fold the dough in half, and pinch the edges closed with a fork. Feel free to decorate the tops with shapes cut out from the extra dough.

Bake the smaller, folded pies at 375F / 190C for 20-25 minutes, or until golden brown.

The flavor is equally good either way. Use whatever shape fits your overall meal strategy. After all, going on an adventure is no reason to be uncivilized.

**VEGAN VARIATION**

The larger pie crusts don't hold up well when oil is substituted for butter, so you're best off sticking to the smaller, folded ones. Replace the filling's butter with coconut oil or vegan margarine. Increase the cinnamon by 1 tsp and add 1 tsp of salt to make up for the flavor difference. The pastry won't bake up into as deep a golden brown, but it'll still be perfectly tasty.

# Porter Cake

Don't be intimidated by the list of ingredients. This isn't fancy Elven baking chemistry. Like most Shire foods, this is good, solid stuff that can handle a lot of improvisation depending on what you happen to have in your pantry. All you really need is some butter, sugar, flour, eggs, a cup of whatever dried fruits you like best, a couple teaspoons of your favorite holiday spices, and a bottle of beer. Think of the ingredient list more as a set of guidelines than a mandate.

You see, Porter Cake was the Victorian working class answer to fashionable city folk's fruit cake. Instead of wasting a good brandy by pouring it over your pudding, a working class cook simply pulled out a pint good, dark, malty beer. Instead of fresh or candied fruits, she'd throw in a cup of whatever dried fruits she had on hand.

While this is delicious hot and fresh out of the oven, it's even better after the flavors have had a couple days to play nicely together. Wrap it up in foil or, if you're feeling extra Hobbity, wrap it in cheesecloth and leave it in a bread box for a couple of days. The alcohol and fat act as a preservative, helping keep the cake fresh at room temperature for up to a week. However, since it smells better every day, good luck making it last that long.

*¾ c / 85 g room temperature butter*
*1 c / 200 g sugar*
*3 eggs*
*1 orange, juice and zest*
*1 tsp baking powder*
*2 ½ c / 320 g flour*
*1 tsp cinnamon*
*½ tsp allspice*
*½ tsp nutmeg*
*Pinch cloves*
*¼ c / 50 g candied citrus peel (orange, lemon, or a mix)*
*¼ c / 85 g cherries*
*¼ c /85 g currants*
*¼ c / 85 g sultanas/golden raisins*
*¼ c / 85 g raisins*
*1 ¼ c / 300 ml Guinness or other porter beer*
*¼ c / 50 g flaked almonds*
*½ c / 110 g packed brown sugar*

If you know you're making a cake tomorrow, soak your assorted dried fruits in ½ cup / 110 ml of porter overnight to help plump them back up. Don't stress if you either don't have the time or prefer not to waste perfectly drinkable beer. Your cake will be fine if you just toss the fruit right in the batter.

When you're ready to make the cake, start by creaming together your room temperature butter, sugar, and eggs. Add the juice and zest of one orange. You may be thinking this is a good time to add some vanilla. That's not on the ingredient list because Tolkien was very serious about keeping new world foods out of the Shire. Both vanilla and chocolate would be unknown to Hobbits.

In another bowl, mix your flour, baking powder, and all the spices.

Roll your moist fruit in the flour mix. If you can get a nice coating of flour on it, that will help keep the fruit from sinking to the bottom of the cake while it bakes.

Once your fruit is all floured up, introduce the flour mix to the butter mix. Take them on a nice little dance around your bowl until they're all mixed up. Once they're happily confused, pour a little beer. Nah, you want these ingredients to party. Pour in all the beer. Keep mixing until the foam dies down.

Generously grease a couple of 9 inch / 22 cm cake pans. Square pans make for easy cutting and dense packing, but you're just as welcome to use round pans or even bake this in two 1-pound loaf pans instead. Regardless of what pan you use, be generous with the butter. This isn't health food.

Pour your batter into the buttery pans and give them a nice shake to help smooth out the crust.

Sprinkle the brown sugar evenly over your cakes. Top that with an even sprinkling of thin flaked almond slices. Use your fingers to press the almonds into the batter gently. This will help prevent them from escaping when you slice the cake.

Bake at 325F / 160C for 45-50 minutes, or until the crust is a dark, crunchy brown and a toothpick inserted in the middle comes out clean.

You'll end up with an incredibly moist, dense cake that has as much in common with a modern fruitcake as a slow baked Sunday chicken does with drive-through nuggets. It's time travel for your taste buds.

**VEGAN VARIATION**

Substitute 1 c / 100 g vegan margarine for the butter. The extra fat helps make up for excluding the eggs. Increase the baking powder to 1 ¼ tsp. Eggs not only bind food together, they also help it rise. The extra baking powder should help keep your vegan cake from going flat. It'll end up a little crumblier than the egg-inclusive version, so put the cooled cake in the fridge for at least two hours to really solidify before cutting.

# Elevenses

Elevenses is like brunch, only with fewer savory dishes.

Think of it as a chance to relax with an assortment of light breads, maybe interspersed with a nice wedge of cheese from time to time. Nothing too heavy - you don't want to ruin your appetite for lunch, after all.

While second breakfast was all about hearty, durable foods you could tuck in a pack and use as adventure fuel, these are more delicate breads, best served fresh and hot from the oven with a dab of butter and fresh country jam.

# Braided Bread Stuffed with Mushrooms, Onions, and Cheese

This hearty bread is practically a meal unto itself. In celebration of Hobbits well-known love of mushrooms, this is stuffed with mushrooms, onions, cheese, and English country herbs. It's best fresh from the oven while the cheese is still runny, but the leftovers are almost as good served alongside supper to help soak up a hearty plate of mutton or venison gravy.

**Dough:**
*1 ½ c / 300 g water*
*1 tbsp active dry yeast*
*4 tbsp / 85 g honey*
*4 eggs*
*½ c oil*
*6 ½ -7 c / 825 - 850 g bread flour*
*1 tbsp coarse salt*
*8 cloves minced garlic*
*1 tbsp fresh rosemary leaves*
*1 tsp fresh basil leaves, minced*

**Filling:**
*2 tbsp butter*
*2 c / 200 g sliced mushrooms*
*2 onions, diced*
*2 c / 250 g shredded mozzarella*
*2 cloves garlic in filling*
*1 tbsp rosemary in each*
*1 tsp basil*
*1 tbsp coarse salt*

To make a loaf, start by dissolving your yeast in the warm water. Feel free to add an extra tsp of honey at this stage to help kick start your yeast.

Walk away for ten minutes. When you come back, the yeast should have bloomed, so it looks like a mushroom cap rising up out of your bowl. It knows its fate.

Mix in the eggs, oil, salt, and the rest of the honey. When you achieve a soupy mass, add the minced garlic, fresh rosemary leaves, and fresh basil. It should smell delicious.

Now mix in the bread flour. Modern cooks with a stand mixer can attach the dough hook and let it knead away for 6-8 minutes. If you want to get a real feel for the period, knead it by hand for 8-10 minutes. The dough should be soft, pliant, and not too tacky.

Form it into a ball, cover it with a clean dishtowel, and let it rise for an hour, or until double in size.

Meanwhile, make your filling. Melt your butter in a large skillet over medium-high heat. Add your onions and cook until they start to brown. You want them to lose a lot of moisture while gaining some flavor. Once the onions start to brown, add your garlic, rosemary, and basil. Keep cooking for another 3-4 minutes, or until the garlic barely starts to brown. Finally, add the mushrooms. You don't want to overcook them. Mix them in and cook for another 4-5 minutes, stirring frequently. Take the pan off the heat and finish it with the coarse salt. Set it aside to cool while the dough continues rising.

Once the dough has doubled in size, punch it down. Flour a clean surface and roll the dough into a rectangle. Put that rectangle on a sheet of parchment paper so you can easily move the finished loaf to a pan. Trim away any rough edges.

Now that you have a trimmed rectangle of dough, mentally divide the rectangle into thirds. The center third is where you place your filling. The outer two-thirds will be cut into braid strips. To give it an attractive, braided top, make neat, even, 1 inch / 2.5 cm wide cuts along each side.

Make a bed of cheese in the middle ⅓ of your bread. Pile the mushroom filling on top of that. Cover the filling with any remaining cheese.

Fold both end pieces inwards, so they cover some of the fillings. To create the braided top, pull the cut edges of dough over the center, alternating sides and tugging tight, so the dough completely covers the filling.

This makes a single, massive rectangular loaf. Slide it onto your largest cooking pan. If you don't have any oversized baking sheets, just slide it into a heavily buttered 9x13 glass baking pan. Either way, let it rise for another hour.

You put this much work into it, so you might as well make the bread pretty. Whisk together an egg and 1 tbsp of water to make an egg wash. Use a pastry brush to paint the surface of the bread. If you'd like, sprinkle another 1 tsp of coarse salt on top.

Bake the bread at 350F / 180C for 35-40 minutes. If the top starts to get too brown, cover it with foil.

Due to the moist interior, the bottom of this bread has a tendency to get soggy if you leave it out overnight. That means it's your duty to consume the entire loaf before bedtime. If you don't have a party of dwarves or a couple teenagers on hand to help you finish it, you can always use the leftovers to make savory mushroom bread pudding for tomorrow's dinner (pg. 116).

# Honey Cakes

Since Tolkien said the Shire was based on nostalgic memories of his childhood, these honey cakes are inspired by late Victorian recipes for twice baked cakes. The second baking hardens the honey glaze in place while firming up the crust, giving them a moist, tender interior and a sweet, crunchy exterior.

*1 ¾ c / 220 g all-purpose flour*
*1½ tsp baking powder*
*½ tsp salt*
*½ c / 115 g room temperature butter*
*½ c / 85 g dried blueberries or currants*
*Zest of 1 lemon*
*¾ c / 200 ml whole milk*
*1 egg*
*¾ c / 255 g honey + ¼ c / 85 g honey, reserved*
*10-12 candied almonds for decoration*

Preheat your oven to 400F / 205C. While the oven heats up, whisk together your flour, baking powder, and salt.

Mix the butter into the flour blend until you achieve a crumbly meal. Once it looks like gravel, add the lemon zest and blueberries or currants. Make sure it's all well blended.

In another bowl, beat the milk, egg, and 3/4 c honey until you get a nice, sloppy mess. Pour that into the crumbly flour blend and mix until the batter is just barely free of lumps. No need to over work it or else you'll burst the blueberries.

Scoop about ⅓ c of the batter into heavily buttered muffin pan wells. You want to use a generous amount of butter instead of liners in order to achieve a nice, crispy crust.

For the first baking, leave them in a 400F / 205C oven for 12 minutes. They'll be ready to take out of the oven when the tops feel solid, but a toothpick stuck in the center comes out a little sticky. If you used enough butter, the cakes should slide right out of the muffin tin. Arrange them 1 inch / 2.5 cm apart on a greased baking sheet.

Gently press a candied almond (or a plain one if you prefer) into the middle of each honey cake then generously drizzle the rest of your honey on top of the cakes. It helps to heat your honey in the microwave for 15-20 seconds to thin it out. Use enough to coat the top and let it drip down the sides. This creates a nice crispy glaze on your honey cakes. Once they're decorated with an almond crown and drizzled in sweetness, let the honey cakes sit for at least 5 minutes so the honey can soak in.

Put the baking sheet back in the oven for 10-12 minutes, or until the tops are a deep golden honey brown.

While they're still perfectly edible days later, if you find yourself the host of an unexpected party, these honey cakes are quick to make and taste amazing fresh from the oven with a bit of jam and clotted cream. They're even better the next day when the crust is nice and crispy and the interior still soft and moist.

# Seed Cake

Many modern readers imagine seed cake to be chock full of sunflower or pumpkin seeds, but it turns out Tolkien grew up on a decadently buttery version of pound cake full of caraway seeds. They have a sweet, licorice flavor reminiscent of a milder, earthier version of anise seeds. You can find them at most Indian groceries. They've been out of fashion in sweets and tea cakes for a couple generations now, which is a darn shame. If you want to indulge in a little armchair time travel, the next rainy day, try curling up with a good book, a hearty slice of seed cake, and a hot cup of milky tea, and you'll feel transported to another era.

*4 eggs*
*¾ c / 180 g butter*
*1 c / 200 g sugar*
*2 c / 250 g flour*
*3 tsp baking powder*
*1 tsp salt*
*¼ c / 30 g almond meal/flour*
*1 ½ tbsp caraway seeds*
*¼ cup / 60 ml whole milk*
*2 1/2 c / 320 g powdered sugar*
*1/2 cup / 120 ml cold water*
*1 tsp almond extract*

Cream the eggs, butter, and sugar. Yes, that's a lot of butter. The Victorians weren't known for eating healthy. In another bowl, whisk together the flour, baking powder, and salt. Once they're well blended, add the almond meal and all-important caraway seeds.

Mix the dry ingredients into your bowl of butter. Splash in the milk. Now give it all a good beating, so everything is well blended. You should achieve something the thickness of brownie batter. Scoop your batter into a well-greased 2-pound cake pan. (You'll need a spatula. This batter is way too dense to pour.) Shake the pan to help settle the batter before baking.

Bake at 350F / 180 C for 50-55 minutes, or until it is both golden brown on top and a toothpick inserted in the center comes out clean. This loaf is so dense it can be deceptive, so make sure to give it that toothpick test.

Let the cake rest in the pan for 20 minutes before removing it. That both lets it cool and reduces the risk of it crumbling when you remove it. If you buttered the pan heavily enough, after 20 minutes, it should slide right out.

The Victorians weren't fans of icing on their cakes. However, if you prefer a little extra sweetness on top, feel free to add a light sugar glaze. Simply whisk the glaze ingredients together. If it's too thin for your taste, add another 1/4 cup powdered sugar. Let the cake cool completely then paint the glaze on top.

Once the loaf has cooled, serve cut it into 1 inch / 2.5 cm slices. It should last 3-4 days in an airtight container, provided you can keep your hands off it for that long.

# Ginger Oat Bread

This dense ginger-oat bread is based on Parkin, a working class Victorian tea bread. If stored in an airtight container, a loaf of this tasty goodness could keep for up to two weeks. In fact, most people preferred to wait until the bread had aged for at least a few days before serving. This gave the ginger and molasses a chance to mellow while the spices infused the bread. It was most often served with apple or pear compote, which really brings out the flavor of the molasses and cinnamon.

Regional variations included adding a mix of molasses and corn syrup (which you wouldn't see in the Shire since corn is a new world food), substituting up to half a cup of beef dripping with the butter or replacing the butter with lard. Since food cost your average working class family ⅔ of their income, cooks in Tolkien's day were pretty practical about using whatever they had on hand. In that spirit, feel free to make your own ginger oat bread with whatever combination of fats and sugars sounds most delicious to you.

2 ½ c / 500g rolled oatmeal
1 c / 250 g milk (cow or almond)
1 ⅓ c / 300g room temperature butter
1 c / 250g sugar
1 c / 250 g molasses (or treacle)
3 eggs
2 ¼ c / 500g all-purpose flour
3 tsp baking powder

3 tsp ground ginger
1 tsp salt
1 tsp cinnamon
½ tsp allspice
½ tsp nutmeg
Pinch cloves

Start by soaking your oats in the milk of your choice. While the oats enjoy their bath, beat the butter, sugar, and molasses until they're dark and creamy. Add the eggs and keep whisking until you have a sweet, soupy mass.

In another bowl, mix the flour, baking powder, ginger, salt, cinnamon, allspice, nutmeg, and cloves. Make sure your baking soda and spices are all well distributed. Otherwise, you risk having a bland, spiceless bite in one edge of the cake and all the cloves in a single bite elsewhere.

Once all your dry ingredients are playing nicely together, dump them into your butter blend. While you're at it, go ahead and add the milky oats. Keep mixing until you achieve a dense, lumpy batter. Spread the batter in a heavily buttered 9 x 13 inch / 22 x 33 cm cake pan or fill three 1-pound loaf pans.

If you're baking it as a single, flat cake, bake at 350F / 180C for 30-35 min, or until the crust is a dark golden brown and a toothpick inserted in the center comes out clean. If you're baking it as a trio of loaves, cook them for 50-55 minutes, checking with a toothpick for doneness before removing.

## VEGAN VARIATION

To make a modern, vegan version, substitute simple period almond milk for the dairy milk and coconut oil for the butter. To make up for the coconut oil's neutral flavor, double the spices and add an extra 2 tbsp of molasses. Instead of eggs, whisk together ½ c ground flax seeds and ⅔ c water. Let that sit until it becomes gelatinous, then add it to the batter in place of eggs. The strong flavor of the cake will hide the flax.

# Leftover Roast Apple Bread

In keeping with the easygoing nature of Elevenses, this is a quick bread you can whip up using nothing but household staples and last night's leftovers.

This is great the first day, but if you happen to have any leftovers tomorrow morning, try toasting a slice and serving it with butter. If you're feeling extra decadent, butter both sides of a thick slice, fry it up in a griddle until it's a deep golden brown, then serve it topped with a smear of Stewed Apples and Prunes (pg. 14) from Breakfast.

*2 leftover Roasted Apples (pg. 130)*
*3 c / 375 g flour*
*2 tsp baking powder*
*1 tsp cinnamon*
*½ tsp salt*
*4 eggs*
*1 c / 200 g sugar*
*½ c / 115 g room temperature butter*
*1 c / 200 ml whole milk*
*1 c / 220 ml heavy cream*

To make this quick bread, start by creaming your eggs, sugar, and butter. Once those are a golden, sugary mass, add the milk and cream.

In another bowl, mix your flour, baking powder, cinnamon, and salt.

Introduce your dry ingredients to your wet ingredients. Keep mixing until the batter is barely lump free.

Now roughly chop up your leftover roast apples along with all their fillings. If you have any pan juice left from roasting the apples, you can add a couple tbsp of it to the batter for extra flavor.

Thoroughly butter up two loaf pans. Spoon a quarter of the batter into one pan. Top that with a quarter of the chopped apples and filling. Add another layer of batter then another layer of apples.

This creates a nice line of apples down the middle. If you prefer yours with the apples a little more integrated, grab a butter knife and weave it back and forth in the batter a couple of times. The goal isn't a thorough mixing. You just want to muddle things up a little.

Bake your bread at 350F / 175 C for 30-35 minutes, or until a toothpick inserted in the center comes out clean.

# Small Adventure Sized Mincemeat Pies

These pies are a great snack for small adventures taken just outside the borders of the Shire. A hunk of bread, a little cheese, and 2-3 of these make perfectly portable Elevenses that's just the right size to tide you over until a civilized lunch back in the comfort of your Hobbit Hole.

In the middle Ages, mincemeat pies included ground beef and suet (beef kidney fat) as well as generous quantities of spices; the new novelty item brought home by Crusaders. By Tolkien's day, the actual meat had disappeared from mince pies, and the spices were a little less aggressive. Suet became the only animal product left in something now rather inaccurately called "Mincemeat." It makes you really wonder about the real origin story behind some of the more graphic British place names.

Suet is particularly hard to find these days. You'll need to ask your butcher directly because it won't be in the case. If you can get ahold of it, you are in for a real treat. Suet adds a wonderfully rich flavor that can't be imitated by any other fat. That said, you can still make perfectly delicious (if not entirely accurate) mincemeat using butter or lard. Vegans can substitute coconut oil. Whatever fat you use, you'll end up with something that tastes like a grown-up Fig Newton sprinkled in pixie dust and spiked with rum.

**Filling:**
*3 large granny smith apples, peeled and cored*
*1 c / 340 g golden raisins*
*½ c / 170 dried figs, chopped*
*¼ c / 85 g dried cherries*
*¼ c / 85 g dried apricots*
*2 tbsp crystallized ginger*
*¾ c / 150 g brown sugar*
*¼ c / 55 g beef suet (if you can find it), butter, or coconut oil (for vegans)*
*1 orange, zested and juiced*
*1 lemon, zested and juiced*
*½ c / 120 ml spiced rum or brandy*
*1 tsp cinnamon*
*½ tsp nutmeg*
*¼ tsp allspice*
*¼ tsp ground cloves*

In Tolkien's day, this recipe represented a massive amount of work in the form of diligent chopping. Today, all that work has been reduced to one simple step. Put everything in a food processor and pulse 10-12 times, less if you prefer a coarser mixture. That's honestly all you need to do. It's almost embarrassingly easy.

If you don't have a food processor but do have miraculous patience, you can always chop all the solids very fine by hand then mix them with the liquids.

Either way, let the final result sit in the fridge for at least 3 days. Thanks to the combination of alcohol and refrigeration, the mincemeat should keep for up to 6 months, so feel free to make plenty of it.

**Crust:**
*3 c / 380 g flour*
*¼ c / 50 g sugar*
*1 tsp salt*
*1 c / 225 g butter (or 3/4 c / 170 g coconut oil for vegans)*
*¼ c / 60 ml water*
*¼ c / 60 ml apple juice*

Mix the flour, sugar, and salt until well blended. Victorian mincemeat crusts included cornmeal/maize flour, but since maize is a new world grain, Tolkien specifically prohibited it from the Shire. Add your fat of choice. If you were able to get ahold of some suet, adding 1-2 tbsp to the crust really enhances the flavor. Use your fingers to really work the fat into the flour mix until you have something that looks like edible gravel. Moisten it up with the water and apple juice until you achieve a dense, sweet pastry dough. Knead it a few times for good measure, then flatten it into a disc, wrap it in plastic, and leave it in the fridge for at least 15 minutes.

Once your dough has chilled, it's time to start assembling your pies. You can always make one gigantic pie and serve it in slices or make portable pies using the same techniques as the hand pies in second breakfast. However, these bite sized mini pies are perfect for either Elevenses or a working man's tea.

Spray a mini cupcake pan with nonstick coating. Once it's greased up, lightly flour your work surface and roll out about ⅛ of the dough. It's easiest if you work in small batches. Aim for a ⅛ - ¼ inch / 3-5 mm thickness. You don't want to make it too thin. This should be a hearty, satisfying couple of bites, not a dainty pastry. Use a round cookie cutter to cut circles from your dough. Tuck them neatly in the mini cupcake tin's holes. Cut away any excess from the top.

Once you've made all your bottom crusts, fill them with about 1 tbsp of refrigerated mincemeat mix. Your mileage may vary depending on the size of your mini cupcake pan. Make sure to leave a little room at the top for the top crusts.

Roll out the last of your dough. Cut out top crusts for your tiny pies. You can use a simple circle or make a thick X of dough, but if you have any mini cookie cutters, leaves, moons, or other autumnal decorations make them look extra fancy for little-added work. Whatever shape you pick, just make sure it doesn't cover the top completely. You want to leave a little room for steam to escape while the pies bake.

Once your pies are filled and topped, pop them in a 400F / 205C oven for 18-20 min or until the tops are golden brown. It may be a struggle, but once you remove them from the oven, let them sit for at least 15 minutes to set.

These are delicious hot, but unlike most baked goods, they taste even better the next morning. That makes them great snacks for Elevenses when adventuring outside the shire.

### VEGAN VARIATION

 Substitute coconut oil or your preferred vegan margarine for the butter and suet. Instead of water and apple juice in the crust, use all apple juice to add to the natural sweetness and flavor. For the filling, increase all spices by 25% and add ½ tsp of salt and 1 tbsp molasses or dark treacle to make up for the missing animal fat flavors. It won't taste the same, but it will still taste delicious.

# Chelsea Buns

Chelsea Buns are the ancestor of what Americans call cinnamon rolls. The two biggest differences are the crust and the icing. American cinnamon rolls are usually baked with the dough touching. Instead of picking one up, you have to cut it out of a pan. This means the edges have the texture of soft, fluffy interior bread. Chelsea Buns are baked sitting individually, so you retain the lovely spiral shape and the entire exterior crisps up.

Americans also like to drown their cinnamon rolls in a dense, sugary, cream cheese based icing which can easily overwhelm the flavors of the bread itself. Chelsea Buns are lightly coated in a thin, protective sugar glaze that gives a small added hint of sweetness without distracting from the bun itself.

**Dough:**
*1 tbsp yeast*
*1 ¼ c / 300 ml warm milk*
*⅓ c / 30 g table sugar*
*2 tbsp room temperature butter*
*1 egg*
*1 tsp salt*
*½ tsp nutmeg*
*½ tsp fresh lemon zest*
*3 ⅔ c / 500 g flour*

**Filling:**
*2 tbsp butter, melted*
*⅓ c / 75 g brown sugar*
*2 tsp ground cinnamon*
*1 tsp fresh lemon zest*
*½ c / 100 g dried mixed fruit (currants, raisins, apricots, or a mix of your favorites)*

**Glaze:**
*2 tbsp milk*
*2 tbsp powdered sugar*

Mix the yeast into the warm milk until it's fully dissolved. Let it bloom for ten minutes. When you come back, it should have developed a nice, reassuringly Hobbity mushroom shaped dome.

Add the sugar, butter, and egg then whisk it all into a milky slurry. Once it's well blended, add the salt, nutmeg, and lemon zest. Once more, give it a hearty stir. Finally, add the flour, half a cup at a time, until you achieve a good, solid dough.

If you have a stand mixer, attach the dough hook and let the machine knead away on low for 6-8 minutes. If you're in the mood to be more traditional, lightly knead the dough on a floured surface for 8-10 minutes, or until the surface develops a nice sheen.

Put the dough into a greased bowl, cover it with a clean towel, and let it rise for an hour, or until doubled in size.

Admire your handiwork for a moment before punching down the dough. Once you're feeling satisfied, spread a handful of flour on a clean work surface and grab your rolling pin, because you're going to roll that neat little ball into a massive rectangle. How massive? That depends entirely on how much clean counter space you have available. Keep it in a 2:1 (length: width) ratio for however much space you have, up to about 3 feet / 1 meter on the long edge. (Shorter than that is just fine.)

Once you have a nice rectangle of dough, mix the cinnamon and lemon zest into the melted butter and paint the entire rectangle.

Next spread your brown sugar over the butter mix, making sure to keep the layer as even as possible.

Finally, spread your mixed fruit over the sugar. Currants are traditional, but you're welcome to use any mix of dried, diced fruit you please.

It's time to turn that rectangle into buns. Carefully roll it along the longest side until, instead of a flat rectangle, you have a long, round tube of dough filled with tasty sweets.

Cut the dough into 1 inch / 2.5 cm wide strips. Arrange them on a baking sheet with at least 3 inches / 7.5 cm of space between them, so they won't touch when they rise.

Once all of your rolls are cut and arranged, cover them with a light, clean kitchen towel and let them rise for another 45 minutes until nearly double in size (60-70 minutes on a particularly cold day. The warmer it is, the faster they rise.)

Bake at 400F / 205C for 20-25 minutes, or until the rolls are golden brown.

While they're still hot, whisk the milk and powdered sugar together into a thin glaze and paint it on top of the steaming Chelsea Buns. If you want a little extra bit of sweetness, you can sprinkle the hot, glazed rolls with an additional ½ tsp coarse sanding sugar.

These are best eaten while still warm. Enjoy them with a smear of fresh butter and a nice cup of tea.

# Luncheon

After cold meals for Second Breakfast and Elevenses, a hearty, warm Luncheon would hit the spot.

Food was much more expensive in Tolkien's day. While wealthy Victorian householders could afford fresh ingredients for every meal, cooks in country villages like those that inspired the Shire were well practiced in magically transforming leftovers over the course of many meals. You'll see that reflected in these Luncheon recipes.

Leftover roast apples from last night's dinner make decadently hearty bread for today's luncheon, which can then be toasted or fried up for tomorrow's breakfast. Last night's mashed potatoes are used to make today's potato cakes while Sunday's roast chicken carcass is recycled into broth for today's simple mushroom soup.

# Steak and Ale Pie

Savory pies were a staple of pub grub. Before the invention of modern restaurants, English taverns and inns traditionally offered set price menus promising all the meat, soup, and bread you could eat. A good, hearty pie not only let them stretch out the expensive meat but also simplified serving so working men could fill up quickly during their brief lunches and cold, tired travelers could quickly get something warm in their belly after a long day on the road.

A pub pie this size could easily feed a party with a dozen hungry dwarves or four teenage boys. Feel free to cut the recipe in half if you're feeding less ravenous hordes.

**Filling:**
*2 1/4 lbs / 1 kg stewing beef, trimmed and cubed*
*½ lb / 250g button mushrooms, quartered*
*½ lb / 250 g carrots, peeled and cut into 1 inch / 2.5 cm chunks*
*2 c / 475ml ale*
*2 ¼ c / 500ml beef stock*
*4 tbsp / 60 g butter*
*¼ lb / 100g bacon*
*2 medium onions, peeled and sliced*
*4 garlic cloves, chopped*
*1 large sprig / 1 tbsp fresh rosemary leaves*
*½ tbsp thyme leaves*
*2 bay leaves*
*1 tsp coarse salt*
*1 tsp fresh ground black pepper*
*2 tbsp flour*
*¼ c / 60 ml cold water*

**Crust:**
*2 c / 225 g all-purpose flour*
*½ c / 120 g softened butter*
*¼ tsp coarse salt*
*1 egg, beaten*
*1 tbsp cold water*

To make the filling, start by frying the bacon in a large skillet until it's crispy. Set the bacon aside on a plate. You now have a pan full of delicious bacon grease. Add the cubes of beef and brown them on all sides. You'll probably need to do this in 3-4 batches to keep from overcrowding the pan. As each batch of beef is browned up, add it to a Dutch oven.

Once your beef is all browned, melt the butter in your skillet. Add the sliced onions and let them cook over medium-high heat for 3-4 minutes, or until they start to soften. Toss in the chopped garlic cloves and keep cooking for another 3-4 minutes or until the garlic just barely starts to brown. Add the sprig of rosemary leaves, thyme, and fresh ground pepper. Keep cooking for another 1-2 minutes to release the flavor of the herbs.

You know, that beef looks lonely sitting by itself. Scrape your onion mix into the Dutch oven to keep it company. While you're at it, add in the carrots, ale, and beef stock.

Bring the mix to a boil. Put a lid on it, reduce the heat down to medium-low, and let it simmer for about an hour and a half, or until the carrots are cooked through, and the steak is tender.

While the steak is cooking, mix up your pastry crust. This simple, dense crust adds amazing flavor - mostly because everything tastes better when drowned in butter. Mix the flour and salt. Now use your fingers to knead the flour into the butter until it resembles coarse gravel. Moisten that up by adding the beaten egg and 1 tbsp cold water. Keep mixing until you achieve a dense dough, then knead that a few times for good measure.

Divide your dough in half. Roll half of it until it's just large enough to cover the bottom of a well-greased casserole dish or cake pan. Use a fork to poke a few holes in the bottom.

After a good 90 minute simmer, whisk together 2 tbsp flour and ¼ c cold water until you have no lumps. Gradually stir that into the stew to help thicken it.

After staring at that fried bacon for the last hour and a half, it's finally time to crumble it all up into the stew. Give the stew a hearty stir, then start ladling it into the casserole dish. Fill it ¾ of the way up. Any more than that and you risk it boiling over and spilling out the side of your dish. If you have any left over, save it for individual pot pies.

Roll the remaining crust into a rectangle. Lay it on top of your casserole dish and pinch the edges closed. Trim off any excess.

Since you already went to all this effort, go ahead and knead the excess trimmed dough back into a ball. Roll it flat and use a small cookie cutter to cut out some attractive shapes. Use the extra dough to decorate the surface of your pie.

Whisk together an egg and 1 tbsp of water. Use a pastry brush to paint the egg wash on the surface of your pie crust. This will give it a lovely golden brown sheen.

Bake the pie at 400F / 205C for 30-35 minutes, or until the top crust is a dark, golden brown.

If you prefer, you can make this a gluten free period stew by simply leaving out the flour thickener and serving it directly in bowls with no pastry crust.

## VEGETARIAN VARIATION

Butter is such an integral flavor that this doesn't transition well into vegan limitations, but you can easily make it vegetarian. Omit the bacon and replace the bacon grease with more butter. Replace the beef broth with vegetable broth and replace the beef itself with more root vegetables. In addition to the potatoes and carrots, try adding some peeled and diced turnips and rutabaga (also known as swede.) When meat was scarce, the only beef in the steak and ale pie might be in the form of broth, so this vegetarian variation isn't far off from what people in Tolkien's youth actually ate.

# Baked Scotch Eggs

This hearty pub grub makes a perfect luncheon for anyone fresh back from a tiring morning adventure. Serve it alongside a hearty crust of country bread and a freshly picked salad, and you won't feel the least bit peckish until afternoon tea.

Scotch Eggs are traditionally a deep fried decadence. However, fat was often very expensive in rural communities, and even when it was available in excess, only wealthy households or taverns had the kitchen technology necessary to boil a whole pot of it safely. In honor of frugal hobbits, I present this more everyday baked version of the fried treat. If you're feeling bold and decadent, you can certainly pop these into your deep fryer instead of baking them and enjoy delicious results.

*3 garlic cloves, minced*
*1 ½ tbsp salt + 1 tsp salt*
*1 tbsp ground black pepper*
*3 1/2 tbsp paprika*
*1/3 tbsp fennel seed*
*1 tbsp savory (or rubbed sage)*
*1 tbsp rosemary*
*2 c / 300 g coarse breadcrumbs (or ground cornflakes if gluten free)*
*6 hard-boiled eggs*
*1 raw egg*
*2 1/4 lbs / 1 kg ground beef, pork, or a mix of both*

Mix the garlic, salt, pepper, paprika, fennel, savory, and rosemary. Add 1 tbsp of the spice mix plus the extra 1 tsp salt to the breadcrumbs and set that aside.

Mix the raw egg and the rest of the spice blend into the ground beef to create a sticky dough. Divide the meat mix into six portions. Flatten them out then wrap the meat tightly around each hard-boiled egg until you have six baseball sized meat wads.

In another bowl, whisk together the raw egg and 1 tbsp water.

Set up an assembly station. You want one bowl with the raw egg, another with the seasoned breadcrumbs, and an aluminum foil lined baking sheet with a meat rack on it at the end. Roll the meatballs in the beaten egg. Once they're nice and sticky, roll them in the seasoned breadcrumbs.

Arrange the breaded scotch eggs on the meat rack. This keeps the Scotch Eggs from sitting in their own juices as they bake. If you don't put them on a rack, they'll end up somewhat greasy, and the bottom crust will be soggy. Bake at 375F / 190C for 45 minutes, turning every 15 minutes.

If you've used properly fatty meat, you'll have a nice pool of seasoned grease beneath your meat rack. Go ahead and sop some up with a hunk of crusty bread. It's delicious.

Serve the Scotch Eggs cut in half with a sprinkle of pepper and a dab of hot mustard.

# Mushroom Soup in Home Made Roasted Chicken Broth

This quick, cheap soup is a great way to warm the belly while also stretching out more expensive luncheon ingredients in case you end up hosting an unexpected party full of rowdy dwarves.

*1 lb / 450 g mushrooms, sliced*
*1 shallot, sliced*
*2 tbsp butter or cooking oil for vegans*
*1 tsp thyme*
*1 bay leaf*
*6 c / 1.4 l chicken or vegetable broth for vegans*
*1 tsp coarse salt*
*½ tsp fresh ground black pepper*

Fetch 6 cups of the broth you made from the carcass of last night's roast chicken (pg. 113) and bring it to a boil. You can also use canned broth, but the flavor just won't be the same. With simple food, the flavor comes from quality ingredients. Whatever broth you use, add the bay leaf, thyme, salt, and pepper.

While the broth comes to a boil, melt the butter in a skillet over medium-high heat. Cook the shallots for 3-4 minutes or until they start to brown. Add the mushrooms and cook them for another 3-4 minutes.

Dump the sautéed shallots and mushrooms into the boiling broth and mix well. Turn off the heat, put a lid on top, and let the soup flavors mingle for 5-8 minutes.

Fish out the bay leaf and serve hot. If you can't serve this immediately, hold off on combining the mushroom mix and hot broth until 10 minutes before serving. If you let the mushrooms soak for too long, they'll turn your soup dark and suspiciously cloudy.

## VEGAN VARIATION

If you have homemade vegetable broth, this is the time to use it. The broth is the real star of this soup, and store bought broth just doesn't pack much punch. In addition to substituting veggie broth for chicken broth and subbing in the cooking oil of your choice (olive works well, even though that would've been virtually unknown in the Shire) increase the oil by 1 tbsp. You want to make up for the natural fats in the homemade chicken broth.

# Pan Fried Tater Cakes with Onions

These tasty, pan-fried bites of potato goodness are perfect for soaking up gravy from your steak and ale pie or stewed rabbit. The key to success is patience. Trust your grandmother's wisdom and walk away for a good ten minutes before flipping them and you'll be rewarded with perfectly crisp, wonderful examples of how common, country people in Tolkien's day often had tastier meals than their wealthier city cousins.

*1 c / 200 g shredded potatoes*
*2 c / 200 g mashed potatoes*
*1 c flour*
*1 large onion, minced*
*½ c / 100 g shredded cheddar (or your favorite cheese)*
*¼ c / 60 ml whole milk*
*2 garlic cloves, minced*
*1 tbsp coarse salt*
*1 tsp fresh ground black pepper*
*4 tbsp softened butter, plus 4-6 tbsp butter for frying*

Peel and grate your raw potatoes. To reduce the starch, soak them in cold water for five minutes. Don't skip this step. It makes a big difference. While the raw potatoes are soaking, mix your leftover mashed potatoes, flour, minced onion, minced garlic, salt, pepper, milk, shredded cheese and softened butter. You should end up with something a little thicker than lumpy pancake batter. Drain your raw potato shreds, give them one last rinse, and mix them into the batter.

Melt a tbsp of butter in a large skillet over medium heat - no hotter! Drop in a heaping tbsp full of batter and use the back of a spoon to flatten it slightly. You should be able to fry 3 potato cakes in a round pan or four in a square one.

Here's the hard part. Once your potato cakes are nice and round, leave them alone. Let them sizzle away over medium heat for about ten minutes. If your first batch starts to burn before 10 minutes are up, turn down the heat.

When you flip the tater cakes, the bottom side should be a lovely dark golden brown. Let them crisp up for another 6-8 minutes on the second side.

Since they are a bit time-consuming, don't be afraid of making two pans at once. Just stagger the flipping. Put down three potato cakes in the first pan. Wait five minutes, put three in a second pan, wait five more five minutes. You can get into a good rhythm of flipping one skillet and adding new batter to the other.

In addition to making great gravy sops, these small, round potato cakes also taste surprisingly good with a sprinkle of coarse salt and a dollop of fresh applesauce.

## VEGAN VARIATION

Peel and dice 3 large potatoes. Boil them in vegetable broth until they're just tender. Substitute this for the mashed potatoes. Instead of milk, substitute ¼ c of the broth you boiled the potatoes in. Double the salt, pepper, and garlic. Substitute the cooking oil of your choice for the butter. Other than that, the ingredients and techniques are the same.

# Lemon and Pepper Baked Fish with Asparagus

Tolkien based the Shire on a rural village outside Birmingham. Readers outside the UK are prone to thinking of the country one big coastline, but Birmingham is a thoroughly landlocked city smack in the middle of England. Tolkien wrote that the country village where he spent some of the happiest years of his childhood wasn't on the train lines. This meant it was wonderfully isolated from what he saw as the worst parts of the industrial revolution. That also meant fresh fish would've been in limited supply.

The nearest port cities would've been around 100 miles away from the Shire. By horseback, that's 3-4 days ride in each direction. With no air conditioning and no travel faster than a horse, your best case scenario is one-week old stinky fish. People certainly would've enjoyed whatever river fish they could catch, but mutton, rabbit, chicken, and occasionally beef would've been their preferred protein.

This easy baked fish dish is more the sort of thing. Hobbits would encounter on an adventure, dining in strange, new and distant lands - dozens of miles away!

*2 filets white fish of your choice (cod, haddock, or whatever is fresh and sustainable) cut no more than ¾ inch / 2 cm thick*
*Juice and zest of 2 lemons*
*2 tbsp melted butter*
*1 tsp rosemary*
*1 tsp thyme*
*1 tsp coarse salt*
*1/2 tsp fresh ground black pepper*
*1 lb / 450 g asparagus, trimmed*

Butter or oil up a baking sheet. Once your pan is prepped, in a large bowl, mix your fresh lemon juice and zest with the melted butter, rosemary, thyme, and coarse salt. You want to use a large bowl because you're now going to dump in your fish and rub the lemon mix all over both sides, preferably without getting it all over your counter. Rub whatever's left all over your asparagus.

Once your fish and asparagus are coated with lovely smelling herbs, arrange your fish filets in the middle of the sheet. Spread your trimmed asparagus in a single layer on either side.

Now grind the pepper directly over the top of your fish and asparagus. If you're a big fan of fresh ground black pepper, go ahead and keep grinding until you've applied a tsp or more. It tastes lovely with the fresh lemon and herbs but was incredibly expensive in Tolkien's day, so going light is actually a bit more authentic.

Bake at 375F / 190C. The thicker the fish, the longer it will take. At the 10 minute mark, stir the asparagus (you mostly want to flip it over) and rotate the pan 180 degrees to make up for any inconsistencies in your oven's internal heat. Put it back in the oven and bake for another 5-10 minutes (for a total of 15-20 minutes) or until your fish flakes easily with a fork.

The real trick to this is making sure everything is about the same thickness. If thick asparagus is in season, get a thicker cut of fish. If your grocer only stocks the thin stuff, opt for less period authentic filets of Tilapia or Swai instead of Haddock or Cod.

If you're still full from Elevenses, make yourself a wonderfully satisfying light meal with a piece of fish, some asparagus, and a bowl of homemade mushroom soup.

# Strawberries and Cream Bread

This moist, decadent spring bread embodies all the simple joys of the English countryside that were lost in the gritty industrialized cities. Rural children were often sent out to collect fresh strawberries, with the adults knowing full well that they'd come home with as many berries in their bellies as in their baskets. The freshly picked berries mixed with this morning's cream and farmhouse butter would make a simple, economical treat beyond the imagination of the children's city cousins. Tolkien spent part of his childhood in both worlds and said his time in Industrial Era Birmingham left him with a keen appreciation of wholesome country food.

*1 c / 200 g sugar*
*½ c / 115 g butter*
*2 eggs*
*2 c / 250 g flour*
*2 tsp baking powder*
*½ tsp salt*
*1 ½ c / 110 g chopped strawberries*
*½ c / 100 g chopped almonds*
*½ c /130 ml heavy cream*

Preheat your oven to 350F / 180 C.

While the oven heats up, cream together the butter, sugar, and eggs. In another bowl, whisk the flour, baking powder, and salt.

Chop up a cup, and a half of fresh berries collected around the Shire and add those to your sugar mix. While you're at it, throw in half a cup of chopped almonds or your favorite nuts to give it a nice texture. Drown that decadence in a cup of heavy cream, because strawberries and cream are delicious together.

Once the fruit and nuts are well integrated, add your flour mix. Beat it until the lumps just barely disappear. You don't want to overwork the dough or mangle the strawberries too badly.

Pour the batter into a heavily buttered loaf pan and bake at 350F / 180C for 50-60 minutes, or until the top is golden brown and a toothpick inserted in the center comes out clean.

This is best served with even more fresh strawberries. Confidentially, if you're feeling a bit anachronistic, it also pairs exceptionally well with either vanilla or strawberry ice cream. Just keep in mind that as a new world ingredient, vanilla (and chocolate!) would be completely unknown in the Shire. They might have seen ice cream, but that treat was only enjoyed by those wealthy enough to afford an ice house to chill it and household servants to make it.

# Stewed Rabbit with Root Vegetables and Herb Dumplings

Until very recently, rabbits were a common source of protein. Before refrigeration, their small size made one rabbit the perfect amount of meat for a single family's meal with no worry about waste or spoilage. It wasn't uncommon for country families to keep chickens and rabbits as both pets and food. Their wild cousins were incredible pests, and many a farmer who'd had his crops eaten away by the fluffy menace felt vindicated sitting down to a nice supper of stewed wild hare.

If you've never tried rabbit, it's a mild, easygoing meat that pairs perfectly with English herbs. If your large local grocery store stocks bison or goat, the odds are good they also occasionally stock rabbit. Some smaller grocers also stock a few frozen rabbits, usually in bottom drawers away from eye level.

**Stew:**
*1 tbsp butter or lard*
*2 onions, diced*
*1 medium rabbit, skinned and quartered*
*2 bay leaves*
*1 tsp fresh ground black pepper*
*2 tsp coarse salt*
*1 tsp dried tarragon*
*1 tsp dried thyme*
*½ tsp dried basil*
*5 c /1-liter water*
*4 large carrots, peeled and cut into large chunks*
*4 medium potatoes, peeled and cut into large chunks*
*1 large turnip, peeled and cut into large chunks*

**Dumplings:**
*1 c /140 g all purpose flour*
*½ c /120 g cold butter*
*¼ c/ 20 g fresh parsley, chopped*
*2 tsp baking powder*
*½ tsp coarse salt*
*½ tsp black pepper*
*Cold water*

Start by peeling your carrots, potatoes, and turnip. Cut the root veggies into equal sized large chunks of around 2 inches / 5 cm.

It's time to get out your trusty Dutch oven again. If you don't have a Dutch oven, use your heartiest stock pot.

Melt 1 tbsp butter or lard over medium-high heat. Once the fat is a liquid, carefully brown your rabbit quarters. Use a pair of tongs to take them out of the pot and add the chopped onion in their place. Cook the onion until it barely starts to brown, no more than 3-4 minutes. Add the salt, pepper, bay leaves, tarragon, thyme, and basil. Mix them in with the onions and keep cooking for another minute.

Add all the water. Give it all a good, hearty stir. Since you're not using broth, you really want the herbs mixed in well. Now return your rabbit pieces to the pot and put a lid on it. Turn the heat down to medium-low. You want to get a nice simmer going. Don't let it come to a heavy boil. Let the hare and herbs simmer for 1 ½ hours, stirring once every 15 minutes or so.

After an hour and a half, add the carrots, potatoes, and turnips. Give it all another good, hearty stir and put the lid back on. Let it keep cooking for another half hour.

Meanwhile, prepare your dumplings. Historically, really decadent dumplings would be made with beef suet, which is a flavorful liver fat. If you have a really good butcher, he can get you some, but few commercial grocers stock it. Instead, we're substituting the cheaper, more commonly available, but still delicious fat of butter.

Mix the flour, salt, pepper, parsley, and baking powder. Now cut the butter into small pieces and add it in. Use your fingers to crumble the butter into the flour mix. Once you've made something akin to parsley flavored gravel, add water, 1 tsp at a time, until you've got just enough to turn the gravel into a soft dough. Don't knead, squeeze, or overwork the dough. If you do, you'll get tough, chewy dumplings instead of soft, fluffy ones. Rip the dough into 8 smaller pieces.

Give your gently simmering stew one more hefty stir. Now carefully drop the 8 dumplings on top of the liquid. Don't fuss with it. Just drop in a dumpling and move along. It doesn't need to be perfect. Get them into the pot as quickly as possible and slap a lid on it.

Clamp the lid down tightly and leave it alone for 20 minutes. Do not raise the lid. If you let the steam escape, you'll ruin your dumplings.

After 20 minutes, take the lid off and admire your handiwork. Use a slotted spoon to lift the dumplings out of the broth carefully. Now, because you're a nice person, fish out the bones. If your broth is too thin, you can boil it uncovered for a few minutes to thicken it up.

Serve each person one hearty scoop of rabbit and veggies with two dumplings. Pour a little extra broth on top to keep it nice and creamy.

If you have unexpected guests, give them each a smaller scoop of soup with one dumpling and serve it with plenty of Pan Fried Tater Cakes (pg 68) and chunks of last night's bread.

# Afternoon Tea

*The Hobbit* has such a timeless feel that it's easy for modern readers to completely miss the book's very first joke. While all classes enjoyed a pot of late afternoon caffeinated goodness, in Tolkien's day, there was a social distinction between high tea and low tea. High tea was more like a working man's early supper complete with plenty of cold cuts, hearty breads, and filling chunks of cheese with whatever sweets the family could afford on the side. Its name came from being eaten around a high table, as often as not, the only table the family owned.

Low tea, on the other hand, was an aristocratic snack time of dainty pastries and tiny pieces of cake served in the parlor, arranged on a low table - hence the name. Working class people who wanted to impress an honored guest would lay out a low tea for them, which Bilbo struggles to do when Gandalf arrives. His frustration comes from having his refined low tea unceremoniously turned into a high tea.

Over time, we've abandoned the concept of low tea, but when *The Hobbit* was first published, readers Tolkien's age and older would've instantly been in on the joke.

In honor of the tea Bilbo tried to set out, these period recipes are all for sweets you might find in a working class household. A handful of plum heavies, a couple gingersnaps, last week's shortbread, and three day old carrot cake would make a respectable offering to impress a dignified guest.

# Hot Cross Buns

Although none of the races of Middle Earth are overtly religious, Tolkien himself once described The Lord of the Rings as "a fundamentally religious and Catholic work." In the same way, there's nothing intrinsically religious about warm, sweet bread stuffed with fruit and glazed with a couple lines of sugar, but Hot Cross Buns are a long standing Catholic tradition.

England had a long history of making bread in special ways to ward off bad luck, evil spirits, and even spoiling. In the 17th century, adding a cross to everyday buns was considered "Popish" and went out of fashion among English Protestants. Bakeries put this bias aside at the Easter season when Catholics and Protestants alike enjoyed Hot Cross Buns on Good Friday.

It's heartbreaking to realize so many of the lush descriptions of food in the Shire were written during England's darkest days of war rationing. During World War II, it wasn't uncommon for English families to save up on their rations for weeks in order to make Hot Cross Buns for a special Good Friday treat. These days, they're available in many bakeries through most of the month of April.

**Dough:**
½ c /120 ml warm milk
1 tbsp yeast
3 tbsp room temperature butter
½ c / 120 ml heavy cream
½ c / 100 g sugar + 1 tsp
1 egg, lightly beaten
1 tsp salt
1 tsp cinnamon
⅓ tsp ginger
1 c / 200 g currants, sultanas (golden raisins) or a mix of both
3 ¼ - 3 ½ c / 425 - 450 g flour
1 tsp lemon zest

**Glaze:**
1 whole egg, beaten
1 egg white
2 tbsp milk
¼ c / 30 g powdered sugar

Completely dissolve the yeast and 1 tsp sugar in warm milk. Since these are normally cold weather treats, the sugar gives the yeast a little extra help getting started on a chilly day.

In 10 minutes, the yeast should be nice and foamy. Add the room temperature butter, heavy cream, sugar, and egg. Beat it all together until the sugar is mostly dissolved. Now add the salt, cinnamon, ginger, and lemon zest. Keep mixing for another minute or so until the spices are well integrated into the liquids.

Now add the flour, ½ cup at a time, until you achieve a dough that's tacky, but not sticky. If you have a stand mixer, attach the dough hook, set it to low, and let the machine do all the work for the next 6-8 minutes. If you're working by hand, spread a little flour on a clean surface and gently knead the dough for 8-10 minutes.

Once you're satisfied with the dough, spread it into a rough rectangle. Add half the currants or sultanas. Fold the dough in half and add the rest. Fold it in half once more. If you mix them straight into the dough, you risk them rising to the surface and expanding into crazy little balloons. Folding them in like this helps keep the fruit anchored in the middle of the buns where it can add sweetness and texture without making the surface look weird.

Pull off golf ball shaped chunks of dough and roll them into a circle. Arrange the buns on a lightly buttered baking sheet, at least 3 inches / 7.5 cm apart, so they won't touch when they rise and bake.

Cover the buns with a light kitchen cloth and let them rise until nearly double in size or about 60 minutes. On particularly cold days it might take a little longer.

Once the rolls have risen, beat an egg until light and frothy. Paint it on the surface of the buns, so they'll come out of the oven nice and shiny.

In Tolkien's day, it was traditional to snip a cross directly into the buns themselves. These days, a lot of people just paint an X on top. The cut buns make a nice effect, plus they're a lot easier to pull apart and share. To make a cross in yours, simply use a pair of kitchen shears to snip two lines in the top right before baking.

Bake at 400F / 205C for 20 minutes, or until the tops are a toasty golden brown.

While they bake, prepare the simple icing. Just mix the egg white and milk together, then gradually add in the powdered sugar until the icing reaches your desired thickness.

Let the buns completely cool before painting on the crosses. Otherwise, the icing will melt off and dribble down the sides. The easiest way to paint on the icing is to squeeze it all into a plastic sandwich bag and snip off the very edge of one corner. You now have an instant, disposable pastry bag you can use to draw neat icing lines.

# Carrot Cake

Carrot Cake's popularity is directly proportionate to the availability of cheap sugar. Sugar and honey were incredibly expensive during the Middle Ages, so sweet root vegetables like carrots and beets made their way into all sorts of desserts. By the time of Tolkien's Victorian childhood, sugar was cheap and readily available in both the country and the city. However, he wrote *The Lord of the Rings* against the backdrop of World War II. Rationing was in effect and sugar was once more rare and precious, meaning carrot cake was once again one of the few treats people could realistically afford.

In fact, at the height of rationing, this cake would have required one adult's entire month of egg rations, three weeks of butter rations, and half a month's sweets rations - if all of that was available in the first place. Tolkien doubtless had plenty of dry, crumbly cake as people stretched their scant sugar, butter, and eggs while still trying to make the occasional festive treat.

*3 1/2 c / 400 g grated carrots*
*½ c / 100 g currants or minced raisins*
*¼ c / 50 g minced golden raisins*
*2 c / 260 g whole wheat flour*
*1 ¼ c / 160 g butter*
*4 eggs*
*¾ c / 150 g sugar*
*3 tsp baking powder*
*1 tsp salt*
*2 tsp cinnamon*
*1 tsp ginger*
*¼ tsp allspice*
*¼ tsp nutmeg*
*Pinch cloves*

Make yourself a nice cup of tea. Since you have a kettle full of hot water anyway, soak your dried fruit in a cup of it.

While the fruit soaks, grate 3 ½ c of carrots. Once they're torn down to shreds, attack them with a chopping knife a few times to mince them into smaller pieces. If you want to save muscle, you can peel the carrots then put them through the fine grind of a food processor.

Cream together the butter, eggs, and sugar. Add the shredded carrots and mix well.

In another bowl, mix the whole wheat flour, baking powder, salt, cinnamon, ginger, allspice, nutmeg, and cloves. Whisk it all together until all the dry ingredients are evenly distributed.

Remember your dried fruit? Drain the water and add the currants and raisins to your flour. By soaking them first, you not only rehydrated the fruit a little but also made the outside nice and sticky. The flour mix should cling to it now. Floured fruits tend to stay put in the batter instead of sinking to the bottom of your cake.

Once your fruit is floured, you're ready to introduce your carrot mix to your flour mix. Beat them wet and dry ingredients together the flour barely becomes smooth. You don't want to overwork the batter.

Pour the batter into half a dozen heavily buttered ramekins or cake tins.

Bake at 350F / 180C for 25-30 minutes, or until the top is a dark, crunchy brown and a toothpick inserted into the middle comes out clean. Alternately, you can pour it into a 9x9 square cake pan and bake for 45-48 minutes.

This medieval inspired carrot cake is less sweet, more dense, and notably spicier than most modern versions. The cream cheese based sugary icing familiar to most American readers is almost unknown in the UK. If you don't like to eat your cake plain, try dusting it with a light coating of powdered sugar or following the British example of pouring a little custard on top.

## VEGAN VARIATION

Since butter rations were scarce during rationing, people regularly substituted margarine. You're following a long standing tradition here. The less standard substitute comes in the form of eggs. Instead of just leaving them out, as most people would've done during rationing, try whisking together ½ c ground flax seeds and ⅔ c water. Let that sit until it becomes gelatinous, then add it to the batter. Double the spices to make up for the flavor of the margarine.

# Plum Heavies

Chocolate and vanilla may seem ubiquitous today, but they're actually both new world beans. That means Tolkien explicitly excluded them from the Shire, even though both flavors were quite popular in Victorian England. Plum Heavies were the cheap, kid's cookies of their day.

Victorian country cooks would knead in a handful of diced plums plus a little extra sugar into any scraps of leftover pastry. Once that was rolled out, they'd cut the pastry into small, child sized bites with a 1-2 inch / 2.5 - 5 cm cookie cutter. Once baked up nice and crunchy, the durable pastry could be stored at room temperature for a week or more. This made them equally good treats for good behavior or parental bribes when you just need to put something in your kid's mouth in order to hush them up.

If you're feeling traditional, Plum Heavies should be made with whatever leftover dough you have around spiked with whatever dried fruit is handy. Chopped raisins and currants were just as popular as plums.

For folks who don't happen to have a lump of leftover pastry dough sitting around after making some second breakfast hand pies or luncheon Steak and Ale pie, here's how to make these rural Victorian treats from scratch.

*2 ½ c / 500 g flour*
*1 c / 225 g butter, softened*
*½ c / 115 g sugar – plus extra for dusting*
*½ c / 115 g minced plums*
*2 tbsp milk*
*1 tsp cinnamon*
*1 egg, beaten to glaze*

Beat the butter, sugar, cinnamon, and milk until you have a dense, fatty mess. Sweeten it up by adding in your minced plums (or other fruit.) Once those are thoroughly integrated, add the flour.

It's time to give up on stirring and just use your hands. Really work the flour into the buttery mix. Once everything is well integrated, knead the dough a few times for good measure.

Roll the dough out to about ¼ inch / 6 mm thickness. Attack the dough with a small, round cookie cutter about 1 ½ inches / 3 cm wide. Remember, the goal here isn't a giant American cookie. It should be just big enough for 2-3 bites. These don't inflate much, so you can squeeze a lot of them onto a cookie sheet. Keep at it until you finally run out of dough.

If you'd like, you can whisk an egg with a tbsp of water for a glaze. Use a pastry brush to paint it on top of the pastry bites. Follow that up with a light dusting of extra sugar.

If you use whole raisins or currants, they have a tendency to rise to the top of the cookies. When baked, they'll look like fruit exploded from the surface. While that's kind of fun, it's also hard to store effectively. You can get around that by properly mincing all your fruit. The sticky cut sides anchor to the pastry, helping the pieces stick in place.

Bake your plum heavies at 350F / 180C for 15-18 minutes, or until the pastry is golden brown and crunchy. They'll turn into a tough mess if refrigerated, so store them in a closed container (like a cookie jar) at room temperature for up to a week.

# Hot Buttered Scones

Forget those crunchy triangles you find at Starbucks. The Victorian scones of Tolkien's day were far more like southern style American biscuits.

Like American biscuits, these are best served fresh, hot, and buttered. Unlike their modern counterparts, they're served at tea time, around 4 p.m., with clotted cream or homemade raspberry jam instead of at breakfast, smothered in gravy.

The creamy interior bears little resemblance to the brick-like pastries masquerading under their name in coffee shops. You can throw together a batch in about half an hour. Try some for yourself and see if you don't prefer your scones Shire-style.

*2 ½ c / 500 g flour*
*1 tsp baking powder*
*1 tsp cream of tartar*
*1/2 tsp sea salt*
*2 ½ tbsp sugar*
*¼ c / 60 g cold butter*
*1 c / 250 ml whole milk*

Whisk together the flour, baking powder, cream of tartar, sugar, and salt. Once they're well mixed, add the butter. Use your fingers to work it into the flour in order to create crumbly edible gravel. The colder the butter, the better your scones.

Once the butter and flour are deliciously crumbly, moisten them up with the milk. Mix the dough until everything is barely combined, then lightly knead the dough a handful of times. You don't want to overwork it.

Spread some flour on a clean work surface. While you're at it, dust your hands. Use them to press the dough, so it's about 2 inches / 5 cm thick. Use a round or fluted round cookie cutter to punch out discs of tasty goodness. You usually see them about 3 inches / 7.5 cm across, but you can use whatever size cutters you own.

Arrange the scones 2 inches / 5 cm apart on a well-greased baking sheet. Don't be shy about the butter. This isn't health food.

While you're at it, melt a little extra butter and paint it on top of your scones. Now that the scones are sitting on a buttery surface and topped with buttery goodness let them rest for about 5 minutes before baking.

Bake at 425F / 220C for 15-20 minutes, or until the tops are a delicious golden brown.

These are best-served piping hot, straight from the oven, with a dab of clotted cream or fresh raspberry jam.

If you decide to take some along on an adventure, remember they won't last more than a day without going horribly stale. Make sure to slather the exterior in butter before toasting day old scones for a light breakfast.

# Shortbread

It's hard to believe something so delicious only has four ingredients. The key to this simple recipe is to embrace your inner love of butter. If you use enough natural dairy goodness, the shortbreads will practically leap off the pan instead of clinging to it like a desperate lover. Save yourself some heartbreak by being generous with the fat.

*1 c / 225 g butter*
*2 c / 260 g flour*
*½ c /100 g sugar*
*½ tsp salt*

Cream your butter and sugar together until they're completely smooth.

Shortbread is excellent on its own, but if you want to add in some extra flavoring agents, now is the time. Lavender and rosemary are perfectly Shire-appropriate additions. At most, add ½ tbsp of either.

Once you've stirred any extra flavors into your buttery goodness, whisk your salt into your flour. Dump the salty flour into your butter mixture. Keep mixing until the flour is completely integrated into the butter. The best method is to give up on the spoon and just reach in there with your hands. Once you have a nice, uniform dough, knead it a few times for good measure.

If you've added any flavoring agents, form the dough into a log, wrap it in plastic, and let it sit in the fridge for a couple of hours so the flavors can mingle. If you don't plan to add any extras, you can either shape it into a log for easy cutting or go ahead and bake it now.

If you want to use a cookie cutter for fun shapes, let your dough come back to room temperature and roll it out to ½ inch / 1.25 cm thickness. If you're not particular about shapes, rolling it into a log and simply slicing off coins certainly saves time. Either way, the shortbreads will taste great.

Arrange your shortbreads 1 inch / 2.5 cm apart on a heavily buttered glass cake pan. The extra butter makes them release even faster.

Bake at 325F / 160C for 18-20 minutes, or until the shortbreads turn a rich golden brown. Don't over bake them or else they'll turn a sickly gray-brown. To preserve the texture, store them in a room temperature an airtight container.

# Country Gingersnaps

Rumor has it Queen Elizabeth I would give visiting dignitaries gold gilded gingerbread versions of themselves around the holidays. Whether or not this is true, crunchy gingersnaps date back to the crusades and were still hugely popular in Tolkien's day. The molasses that make the cookies so distinctive not only used to be cheaper than sugar but its strong flavor also helped cover up impurities in cheaper, coarser grinds of flour, making these a common country tea biscuit.

*1 c / 225 g butter*
*3/4 c / 150 g sugar*
*1 1/4 c / 254 g molasses (black treacle)*
*1 egg*
*2 c / 250 g white flour*
*2 c / 260 g whole wheat flour*
*1 tsp baking powder*
*Zest and juice of 1 lemon*
*3 tbsp cinnamon*
*1 ½ tbsp ginger*
*½ tsp cloves*
*½ tsp salt*

Preheat your oven to 350F / 180C.

Cream together the butter, sugar, molasses, and egg. Add the zest and juice of one lemon.

In another bowl, mix the flour, baking powder, cinnamon, ginger, cloves, and salt.

Such delicious ingredients shouldn't be kept apart. Mix the spicy flour blend into the creamy butter and keep stirring until the mix is free of lumps.

Generously lubricate a baking sheet with butter.

Roll 1 inch / 2.5 cm balls of dough between your hands. Arrange them 2 inches / 5 cm apart on the cookie sheet. Pierce the tops with a fork.

Bake at 350F / 180 C for 10-12 minutes or until the cookies are dark brown.

Leave them on a rack to cool completely. Once cool, they should be crunchy all the way through. If kept in a dark, airtight container, they can stay crunchy and delicious for a couple of weeks, if the batch lasts that long.

# Bannocks

Bannocks can mean anything from an uncut circle of scones to a fluffy fruit cake to these dense, wholesome, country oatcakes. While wealthy households might limit their tea time treats to pastries and delicate sandwiches made from fine white flour, hearty oat Bannocks were more of a working man's alternative - something solid enough to tide you over until dinner but not so sweet or heavy it would ruin your appetite, with just enough spice to highlight a good cup of tea.

*1 c /140 g whole wheat flour*
*3 tbsp baking powder*
*1 tbsp salt*
*½ c / 100 g sugar*
*2 tbsp cinnamon*
*1 tbsp allspice*
*½ tbsp nutmeg*
*½ tbsp cloves*
*1 c / 85 g rolled oats*
*1 c / 240 ml whole fat milk or almond milk for vegans*
*butter for frying*

Mix the flour, baking powder, and salt in a large bowl. Make sure the baking powder is evenly distributed in the salt or else you'll end up with unevenly cooked bannocks.

Now add the sugar, cinnamon, allspice, nutmeg, and cloves. Mix the sugar and spices until everything is well blended. Next, add in the oats and give them a good mix.

Get it all wet by adding the milk. Stir it just enough to make the lumps disappear. You don't need to over work this batter.

Heat a large cast iron skillet or griddle over medium heat. You want to cook these low and slow to avoid burning. Smear the bottom with a generous coat of butter. Honestly, the easiest method is to just rub the stick across the surface of your hot pan.

Ladle in ¼ - ⅓ cup of batter. You can make larger bannocks, but for afternoon tea, the goal is to make small cakes no wider around than a saucer. You should be able to comfortably fit three at a time into a round skillet or four onto a square griddle.

Fry for 3-5 minutes per side, or until they're a dark golden brown.

These are best served warm with a nice cup of milky tea. If you want to make them up in advance, you can reheat them without burning the surface by arranging a single layer on a lined baking sheet and popping them in a 400F / 205C oven for 5-6 minutes, or until warmed through but not yet overly crispy on the outside.

## VEGAN VARIATION

If you're entertaining travelers who don't eat meat, simply substitute your favorite milk alternative (almond milk tastes particularly good in this context) and add 1 tsp vegetable oil to the batter to make up for the lost milk fat. Instead of butter, grease your pan with a swipe of vegetable oil. You'll end up with a wholesome vegan tea time treat.

# Supper

If you're in the mood to start a rollicking argument without resorting to typical subjects like religion or politics, ask people to define the difference between supper and dinner. Whether you're in the UK or the US, you'll get five opinions for every four people (because at least one will have multiple definitions.)

This lack of distinction was just as strong in Tolkien's day, which made including both supper and dinner in the list of a Hobbit's daily meals even funnier. They didn't pick between the two. They had both. It's amusingly decadent now, but to readers trying to stretch their ration books, a world where everyone ate two hearty evening meals each night with plenty of meats and sweets would've been as fantastical as a world filled with elves and dwarves.

# Stuffed and Roasted Mushrooms

No hobbit meal is complete without a mushroom dish. These stuffed, roasted mushrooms make a great main course for nights when you're too tired from adventuring to make a rack of lamb or roast a chicken.

In middle-class Victorian households, stuffed vegetables were a way to make a meal look a little fancy while also being economical. Instead of a pauper's dinner, all it took as a little creativity to turn leftover sausage from breakfast, last night's bread crusts, and a few herbs into an elegant meal.

*4 large Portabella mushroom caps*
*1/2 tbsp butter*
*1 c / 200 g homemade Country Sausage (pg. 15) or vegan sausage crumbles*
*1 medium onion, diced*
*1 clove garlic, minced*
*1 tsp salt*
*1 tsp dried herbs (rosemary or basil)*
*½ tsp fresh ground pepper*
*1 egg, beaten*
*1 1/2 c / 270 g dried breadcrumbs + 4 tbsp reserved (substitute ground cornflakes if gluten free)*
*½ c shredded mozzarella cheese (optional)*

Gently wash the mushroom caps and remove any remaining bits of stem. Let them sit out on a rack to dry while you brown the sausage.

Melt ½ tbsp of butter in a large skillet over medium-high heat. Cook your breakfast sausage until browned through. Once fully browned, add it to a mixing bowl. In the same skillet, add your diced onion, minced garlic, dried herbs, salt, and pepper. Cook for 3-4 minutes, or until the onion is translucent and the garlic starts to brown. Add it to the mixing bowl full of sausage.

Once the mix is cool enough to touch, add the beaten egg. Use your hands to knead the sausage, vegetables, and herbs together with the egg binder. Once they're all mixed, add all but 4 tbsp of breadcrumbs and keep mixing until the crumbs have soaked up a lot of the moisture.

Divide the mix into four parts. Gently press each one into a mushroom cap, taking care not to split the mushroom.

Sprinkle each mushroom with 1 tbsp of reserved breadcrumbs. If you'd like, you can also add a couple tablespoons of shredded cheese.

Bake at 350F / 180C for 15 minutes-18 minutes. Let cool slightly before eating.

If you're having a grand meal, serve one of these alongside one chop from your roast rack of lamb, so everyone feels like they had a hearty, somewhat grand main course. You'll save money while also looking quite fancy.

For a more modest Shire inspired meal, serve these alongside mashed potatoes, green peas cooked with rosemary, and a hunk of fresh bread

## VEGAN VARIATION

Substitute frozen vegan sausage crumbles for the breakfast sausage. Since most fake vegan meats are entirely fat free, cook the meat substitute in 2 tbsp of your favorite fat. When mixing the cooked crumbles with the breadcrumbs, onion, and seasoning, add an extra tablespoon of fat for both binder and texture. Leave out the egg entirely. If you want to add a little vegan cheese as a topping, wait until the last five minutes of cooking. Non-dairy cheese substitutes don't melt - they burn.

# Roast Rack of Lamb

*1 Frenched rack of lamb with 8 ribs*
*1 tbsp cooking oil*
*2 cloves garlic, minced*
*1 tbsp fresh rosemary leaves*
*1 tsp fresh thyme*
*1 tsp kosher salt*
*½ tsp fresh ground black pepper*
*1 tbsp sherry or brandy*
*½ tsp apple cider vinegar*
*½ tsp dark mustard*

Mix everything but the lamb until you have a thick paste. Trim the rack of lamb of excess fat. Leave a layer no more than 1 inch / 2.5 cm thick. Rub the spice paste all over the meat. You can now either let it rest on the counter for two hours until it reaches room temperature or wrap the whole thing in plastic and put it back in the fridge to marinate overnight. If you do, take it out two hours before you're ready to bake. It's important you let the meat return to room temperature before baking. If you don't, you could end up with burned fat, a raw center, and overall uneven badness.

When your nicely crusted lamb is at room temperature, preheat your oven to 400F / 205C.

Put a roasting rack in the bottom of a pan that's not too much bigger than the rack itself. Arrange the rack of lamb fat side up/bone side down in the middle of the pan. Since you probably have less practice roasting a lamb than most Victorian cooks, you might want to insert a meat thermometer into the thickest part of the meat, so you'll know when your lamb is done.

Roast the lamb for 7-8 minutes then reduce the temperature to 300F / 150C. Cook for another 7-15 minutes, depending on how done you like it. For rare lamb, pull it out when the internal temperature reaches 125F / 52C. If you prefer medium rare, let it cook until it reaches 135F / 57C. You don't want to leave it in much past that or else instead of a lovely juicy cut of meat, you'll end up needing a hacksaw to get through it all.

Residual heat will keep cooking the meat, so seriously, don't leave it in the oven for more than 22 minutes total. As soon as you take the rack out of the oven, baste it with its juices. Remove the rack to a plate and wrap it in foil (or, if you want to be more period, put it on the counter, flip over a clean pan, and put it over the lamb to keep it warm. Let the meat rest for 20 minutes.

While the lamb rests, put the roasting pan over your oven burners. (If you didn't use a burner-safe pan, do your best to scrape all the juices and lovely crunchy bits out of the pan and into a skillet.)

Over medium heat, deglaze the roasting pan with your sherry. Stir frequently to get up all the good bits. Add the cider vinegar and dark mustard and keep stirring until you have a thick, gloriously fatty gravy.

Once the lamb has rested for 20 minutes, cut it into four thick chops if you're feeling generous or eight smaller chops if you're hosting unexpected company.

# Home Made Lamb Broth

Lamb chops make especially delicious broth, so when you're cleaning up the plates after dinner, make sure to save the bones.

*8 leftover lamb rib bones*
*any leftover fat and meat*
*2 carrots*
*2 celery sticks*
*2 sprigs of rosemary*
*1 onion*
*1 bay leaf*
*1 tsp coarse salt*
*2 tbsp apple cider vinegar*
*enough water to fill ¾ of your stock pot*

You can just throw the bones and fat into a big pot of boiling water with some carrots, celery, onion, and kitchen herbs. However, if you really want to get the most flavor, you want to roast the bones themselves.

If your guests didn't pick the bones clean, go ahead and try to get as much meat off the leftovers as possible. Save that to use in tomorrow's Mushroom and Beef Hand Pies (pg. 31) for Elevenses (subbing in leftover lamb is delicious) or set it aside as a Boxty topping (pg. 123) for dinner.

Preheat your oven to 375F / 190C. Once it's warmed up, arrange the bones in a single layer on a large baking sheet and roast them for 15 minutes. Flip the bones, then roast them for another 15, for a total of 30 minutes. This may seem pointless since you've already fully cooked the meat, but that extra step adds an amazing amount of flavor to the final broth.

Meanwhile, fill a large crock pot ¾ of the way with hot water. No, this isn't an authentic period technique. Your roasted bone broth needs a good 24 hours of simmering to really leach out all the flavor. If you're comfortable leaving a pot on the stove for that long, then you probably spend a lot of time in the kitchen and know how to look after it properly. For most people, though, crockpots are a miraculous safety invention that lets them use low and slow heat without fear of their house burning down while they're at work. If it helps, name your crockpot George and pretend it's a dutiful member of the family patiently watching the pot for you.

While the bones are roasting, cut your carrots, celery, and onions into quarters and add those to the crockpot. Leave on the onion skin. While you're at it, throw in the bay leaf, rosemary, and salt. Put the lid on and leave it on high while the bones roast.

Once your bones are done roasting, they should be beautifully dark golden brown, this and the onion skin, add a lot of the color to your final broth. Dump your bones into the crockpot, splash them with the apple cider vinegar, and fill the pot ¾ full of water. Make sure to leave an inch or two at the top, so it doesn't bubble over.

Give it all a good stir, put a lid on the crockpot, and reduce the heat to low.

Now for the hard part - leave it alone for at least a day. Every time you open the crockpot, you add to the total necessary cook time. Just let it simmer away.

Once you can't take the glorious scent anymore (try to hold out for at least a day) line a colander with 4 layers of cheesecloth and strain out all the solids. Go ahead and throw the solids away. You've reached all the flavor left in them.

You should have a dark, fragrant broth that smells divine. In Tolkien's time, the elderly, injured, and ill would frequently be given a cup of warm bone broth as a restorative. It's full of protein, some tasty fat, and valuable minerals. You can drink it on its own or use it as a base for soups and stews. If you don't have an immediate use for it, let it cool overnight in the refrigerator then freeze it in usable sized chunks.

## Roasted Asparagus

Due to its cost, asparagus was often called the king of vegetables and the vegetable of kings. If you've ever thought it looks a lot like a line of trees marching across your plate, you're right. Asparagus is actually a fast growing shrub that needs to be harvested twice a year while the shoots are still small. Otherwise, the shrub will overtake your garden and transform from a tasty vegetable into a woody menace. However, the woody fibers make it a great vegetable for roasting. It can stand a lot of heat and a fair amount of moisture without breaking down, which means you can add it to a hot oven without it turning into a gross, mushy paste.

This recipe is a great way to use up the residual heat from a roast rack of lamb or roast chicken. You can throw this in the oven while the meat rests and have both hot and ready for the table at the same time.

*1 lb / 450 g thin asparagus*
*zest of 1 lemon*
*1 tbsp lemon juice*
*½ tsp fresh ground nutmeg*
*1 tsp coarse salt*
*2 tbsp melted butter, divided*

If you've been cooking at a lower temperature, turn your oven up to 400F / 205C.

Coat the asparagus in 1 tbsp butter. Once coated, spread your stalks across a baking sheet in a single layer. Slide the baking sheet in the oven and let it cook for 5 minutes (if you like your asparagus firm. If you prefer it more tender, leave it in for 7 minutes.) Pull it out of the oven and quickly turn the stalks. Return the asparagus to the oven for another 5-7 minutes, depending on your preferred level of doneness.

While you wait for it to finish cooking, mix the remaining 1 tbsp melted butter, 1 tbsp lemon juice, coarse salt, and fresh ground nutmeg. Drizzle the asparagus with seasoned butter as soon as it comes out of the oven. It's now ready to join your main course on the table.

If you're adventuring away from home, this recipe works equally well on an outdoor grill.

**VEGAN VARIATION**

Replace the butter with the oil of your choice and add another pinch each of nutmeg and salt to make up for the difference in flavor.

# Venison Cobbler

In the United States, cobbler usually means a dessert topped with a crumbled butter and flour topping as a substitute for pastry crust. In Tolkien's day, Cobbler meant any sort of pie - sweet or savory - topped with big round pastry "cobbles" instead of enclosed in a full pastry crust. This was primarily done for economic purposes to help stretch out expensive fats like butter.

To Victorians, venison was the king of meats (the far less expensive beef was often passed off as venison in pub dishes), and so after buying a rich cut of meat, there wasn't always enough money left over for a dense, buttery crust. The cobbler was an economical cook's compromise.

If you're on a budget and need to stretch things further, you can substitute 1 pound/ ½ kg of peeled potatoes, turnips or a mix of both for a pound of the venison. You'd be following in a fine tradition of thrifty innkeepers stretching a little meat to a lot of people.

**Filling:**
*2 tbsp butter*
*2 large onions, peeled and sliced*
*2 celery sticks, chopped*
*4 carrots, peeled chopped*
*3 lbs / 1.3 kg venison shoulder trimmed of fat and cut into 1 inch / 2.5 cm cubes*
*2 ¼ c / 500 ml dark ale*
*1 c / 235 ml beef broth*
*2 tbsp flour*
*½ tsp Worcestershire sauce*
*1 tsp mustard powder (not prepared mustard)*
*1 tbsp thyme*
*2 tsp coarse salt*
*½ tsp fresh ground black pepper*
*3 tbsp redcurrant or cherry jelly*
*2 bay leaves*

**Topping:**
*3 ¾ c / 480 g flour*
*1 ½ tbsp baking powder*
*1 ½ tsp salt*
*1 tsp thyme*
*½ c / 115g butter*
*1 ¼ c / 300ml whole milk + 1 tbsp*
*1 egg*

Start by making the cobbler topping. Instead of a full pastry crust, you're essentially making savory biscuits which will be a crunchy golden brown on top and full of brothy flavor on the bottom.

Mix the flour, baking powder, salt, and thyme in a large bowl. Cut your butter into cubes and work it into the flour until it achieves the texture of gravel. Now moisten that gravel into a dough by adding the milk, a little at a time, until you end up with a dough similar to American biscuits or Hot Buttered Scones (pg. 86).

Knead the dough a couple of times for good measure, then cover it with a towel and set it in the fridge while you make the cobbler filling.

Preheat your oven to 400F / 205C.  While the oven heats up, melt the butter in a large skillet over medium-high heat. Gently fry the onions and celery for 4-5 minutes, or until the onion barely starts to brown.

Add the browned onions and celery to a rectangular baking pan. Now add the cubed venison (or beef, if you're feeling thrifty) to the skillet and brown it in batches. Don't overcrowd the pan.

When the venison is browned, send it to join the onions in your baking pan. Add the cubed carrots to keep it company.

Whisk the flour into the beef broth until it's completely dissolved and free of lumps. Now mix in the Worcestershire, mustard powder, thyme, salt, and pepper. Once those are well blended, add the red currant or cherry jelly and keep whisking until you achieve a thick, sweet broth.

Modern cooks may be tempted to leave out the jelly, but you'll miss it if you do. The small quantity adds a hint of sweetness and a subtle background flavor that balances out the bitterness of the ale. Speaking of which, once your jelly is mixed into the broth, pour in the ale and give it all a casual stir. Drop in the bay leaves.

Go back to your pan of meat and veggies. Give them all one more good stir before gently pouring the liquids over the solids. Shake the pan a couple times to settle everything.

It's now time to top it with the "cobblers." Fetch your dough from the fridge and use your hands to press it down until it's about 1 inch / 2.5 cm thick. The cobbles will inflate in the oven, so you don't want them to be too thick.

Use a 3 inch / 7.5 cm round cookie cutter to cut out your cobbles. Honestly, you're welcome to use any fancy shaped cookie cutter you'd like. Hexagons look particularly fetching, as do overlapping diamonds. The point is to cover the entire surface in evenly sized increments in order to make a nice presentation. The easiest way to do this is to overlap each cobble slightly, so it looks more like roofing shingles than street paving stones.

Whisk your egg and remaining 1 tbsp of milk together until smooth. Very carefully paint the glaze over the topping.

Carefully place your dish in the oven. (Try not to slosh too much broth over the top of the cobbles.) Bake for 30 minutes, or until the topping is golden brown and the interior is bubbly.

Take it out of the oven and let the cobbler sit for at least 10 minutes to cool and settle before serving. Make sure your family admires your handiwork before scooping out a cobble or two and a healthy mound of filling onto everyone's plate.

# Rosemary Skillet Peas

Peas are a classic English vegetable that has been that has been horribly maligned due to the cruel arts of preservation. No one in the Shire would understand your hate because their peas were fresh, crisp green orbs that popped satisfyingly with each bite.

It's very difficult to find fresh peas in the grocery store these days (though if you can, you really should give them a try) so this recipe relies on their closest relative, the frozen version. Do not, under any circumstances, make this recipe using the mushy gray mass that plops out of a can. This simple recipe is meant to be a celebration of the goodness you'd find in an English garden, not a funeral dirge for all that was lost to the horrors of canning.

*2 c / 200 g frozen green peas*
*3 tbsp butter*
*1 tbsp dried rosemary*
*1 large clove of garlic, minced*
*2 tsp coarse or kosher salt*

Melt the butter in a large skillet over medium-high heat. Once the butter is melted, add your frozen peas and give them a good stir, so they're completely coated. Cook your peas, stirring often, for 5-6 minutes, or until they're completely thawed and warmed through but not yet soft or mushy.

Sprinkle the rosemary, garlic, and salt on top. Give it all a good stir and continue cooking for another 2-3 minutes or until the garlic barely starts to brown.

If you add the rosemary and garlic too soon, they'll burn by the time the peas are fully cooked. You want them in the butter long enough to add flavor without any tragic consequences.

This recipe can be easily doubled if you're serving plenty of guests or your well-trained family really loves their vegetables.

## VEGAN VARIATION

Simply substitute the cooking oil of your choice for butter. Since the butter does add flavor as well as fat, you might want to add in a second clove of minced garlic and another pinch of salt.

# Rustic Apple Tart

A rustic apple tart is a perfect pantry staple to have on hand if one happens to be friends with wizards. It's fancy enough to feel celebratory yet easy enough you can honestly claim it was no trouble. Better yet, the vegetarian ingredients can be safely left out at room temperature for several days with nothing more than a clean cheesecloth draped on top to keep pests and dust at bay.

*1 batch sweet pastry crust (from the Apple Hand Pies on pg. 36)*
*4 tbsp quince jelly (fig or black cherry make acceptable substitutes)*
*1/2 c / 100 g sugar*
*1 tsp ginger powder*
*1 tsp cinnamon*
*½ tsp nutmeg*
*pinch cloves*
*pinch salt*
*finely grated zest of 1 lemon*
*6 tart green apples, peeled, cored and sliced into thin wedges*
*1 tbsp molasses (or treacle)*
*1 tbsp hot water*
*2 tbsp butter*

Country cooks were well skilled at using the same ingredients and techniques in interesting ways. Rather than conjuring a whole new type of crust, this uses the same sweet pastry dough as the Apple Hand Pies (pg. 34) in the chapter on Elevenses. Instead of enclosing a bunch of little pies, so they'll withstand a small adventure, you're going to serve this rustic beauty open faced as the last bite of supper.

Roll out the crust, so it's a large, 9-10 inch / 22-25 cm circle. Trim away the edges. Rather than throw away the extra dough, try turning it into a batch of Plum Heavies. (pg. 84) for tomorrow's Afternoon Tea.

Butter a baking sheet and arrange the neatly trimmed crust in the middle. (If you're afraid of the tart losing shape during baking, you can arrange the crust in the middle of a spring form pan. You'll still have a rustic, open-faced look when you're done without the distinctive pie-pan shape.)

Spread your quince jelly in the middle. If you can't get ahold of quince jelly, you can always substitute fig or black cherry jellies. The flavors won't be identical, but they'll still be true to the limitations Tolkien placed on the Shire while also tasting wonderful. The outer 3 inches / 7.5 cm will be folded up and around the tart, so leave that area as clean as possible.

Mix the sugar, ginger, cinnamon, nutmeg, cloves, salt, and lemon zest. Once the sugar and spices are well blended, add the green apple slices and toss them until every apple slice is well coated. Thin your molasses (or treacle) out with the hot water and drizzle that on top of the apple slices, tossing once more to ensure all the apples are as evenly coated as possible.

Neatly arrange your well-coated apple slices over the quince jelly. Once you have an even coating of apples, cut the butter into cubes and dot it over the surface of the fruit.

Carefully fold the crust upwards and inwards to keep the interior from escaping. You can either finish the crust by painting it with an egg wash to make it shiny or keep it rustic and add a little flavor by dusting it with ¼ c / 50 g sugar mixed with 1 tsp cinnamon for a little extra shine, sweetness, and crunch.

Bake your tart at 350F / 180C for 25-30 minutes, or until the exterior is a deep golden brown and the interior apples just start to brown at the edges.

You'll want to dig in as soon as it comes out of the oven, but resist your natural urges and let the tart settle and cool for half an hour before serving. It's fantastic on its own but even better with a dab of clotted cream.

Whatever is left of your tart after supper will stay perfectly good for a couple of days at room temperature. It makes a great cold breakfast the next morning or a nice treat to have on hand in case of visiting wizards.

**VEGAN VARIATION**

This tart is a couple tablespoons away from being accidentally vegan. Take it the rest of the way by substituting vegan margarine or coconut oil for the butter. Don't exclude the fat completely or you'll end up with something that looks and smells great, but just doesn't have the right mouth feel.

# Lavender and Lemon Bread

This easy dessert bread will leave your home smelling like an English garden. If you're feeling extra decadent, try substituting heavy cream for the milk. If there's any left after dinner, try smothering a thick leftover slice with butter and toasting each side in a skillet for a quick breakfast. The texture change from toasting does surprisingly delightful things to the flavor and will make you completely forget that you're eating leftovers.

**Batter:**
½ c / 115 g butter, softened
1 c / 400 g sugar
3 eggs
zest of ½ lemon
juice of ½ lemon
⅔ c / 155 ml whole milk or almond milk
1 ½ tbsp dried lavender flowers
2 c / 260 g flour
1 tsp baking powder
½ tsp salt


**Glaze:**
1 tbsp dried lavender flowers
zest of ½ lemon
juice of ½ lemon
1 c / 130 g powdered sugar

Preheat your oven to 350F/180C.

Cream together the butter and sugar. Beat in the eggs, lemon juice, and lemon zest. Once you have a thick, delicious smelling paste, mix in the milk and lavender flowers until all the liquid ingredients are smooth. Let the mix rest for 1-2 minutes, so the lavender will have a little time to absorb some moisture.

Meanwhile, whisk together your flour, baking powder, and salt in another bowl.

Once you've decided the lavender has rehydrated enough, add your dry ingredients to the wet ingredients and mix it all into a heavy batter.

Butter the heck out of two loaf pans. This isn't health food. The butter will both add flavor to the crust and, more importantly, help the bread slide out easily.

Divide the batter equally between the pans and bake your loaves at 350F / 180C for 40-45 minutes, or until the top is a light golden brown and a toothpick inserted in the center comes out clean.

While the loaves bake, prepare your topping by whisking the powdered sugar and lemon juice together until free of lumps. Add the lavender flowers and lemon zest. If the mix is too thin for your taste, you can add more powdered sugar 1 tbsp at a time until it reaches your desired thickness. Remember, the goal here is a light glaze that will soak right into the bread, not a heavy icing.

When the bread comes out of the oven, immediately start jabbing the top with a sharp tined fork. Don't rake into it. You just want to create some subtle holes in the crust so the icing can penetrate.

When you decide you've punctured your bread enough, pour half the glaze over each loaf. Let the loaves sit in their pans for at least 10 minutes while the bread cools, and the glaze soaks into the top. Use a butter knife or thin spatula to loosen the sugar coated sides. If you used enough butter, the loaves should now slide right out of the pans. If you want neat, presentable slices, let the bread cool completely before slicing. Confidentially, it's worth giving up a little presentation to rip into this while it's still warm.

+

Most of the Supper recipes could be made in less than 90 minutes. Since Dinner was the last Hobbit meal of the day, it's a fitting place for the slowest, most labor intensive recipes.

These dishes may take longer to cook, but they make up for it by being a lot less expensive. A whole chicken is not only more affordable than a rack of lamb, but also provides more meat. Oxtails are not only a small fraction the price of venison, but you can also make a delicious broth from the bones. These cheaper cuts of meat, which were common in Tolkien's day, have gone out of fashion in favor of more expensive boneless, skinless fillets with low fat and fast cooking times.

Some rainy Sunday when you have more time than money, it's well worth indulging in one of these classic dishes. While your home fills up with the tasty aromas of an earlier time, you can indulgently curl up with a good book that starts in a hole in the ground.

# Sunday Roast Chicken

A single roast chicken could feed a small family for days. On Sunday night, the parents might have a thigh each while the kids got a drumstick. The next day, everyone would have slices of cold chicken breast with plenty of pickles, mustard, and a chunk of bread. Once all the meat was gone, the rest of the carcass would go into a pot to be turned into broth for soup.

*1 whole roasting chicken*
*½ c / 115 g room temperature butter*
*5 tbsp fresh garden herbs, minced*
*5 cloves garlic, minced*
*2 tsp coarse salt*
*1 whole head of garlic*
*2 large sprigs of rosemary*
*2 ¼ lbs / 1 kg carrots, peeled and cut into 2 inch / 5 cm chunks*
*2 ¼ lbs / 1 kg potatoes, peeled and cut into 2 inch / 5 cm chunks*

Preheat your oven to 475F/245C.

While your oven heats up, mince five tbsps of your favorite fresh garden herbs. If you're not sure what to use, try 2 tbsp rosemary and 1 each of basil, thyme, and marjoram. Don't let that limit you, though. Use whatever grows in your corner of the Shire. If herbs are out of season, you can also substitute 2 ½ tbsp of any pre-mixed herb blend.

Mix the minced herbs with the butter, minced garlic, and coarse salt.

Once you've achieved a nice, chunky herb butter, set it aside. Now peel your carrots and potatoes. You can also add other root vegetables common to the Shire such as turnips or rutabaga (also known as swede). Just make sure they're peeled and cut into 2 inch /5 cm chunks, so all the vegetables will cook evenly.

Spread an even layer of peeled, cubed vegetables in the bottom of a roasting pan.

Now it's time to deal with the bird itself.

Thoroughly rinse the interior and exterior of your chicken in cold water. Remove any gizzards or other internal organs. Use paper towels to pat it dry. A dry chicken bathed in butter will produce a nice, crispy skin. A wet chicken, on the other hand, will end up with limp, soggy skin. Do yourself a favor and dry it up.

Cut your whole head of garlic in half horizontally. Rub it all over the interior of the bird. This not only adds flavor but also has a mild antiseptic effect. This combination of flavor and sanitation is why people commonly rub cut lemons on the interior of a chicken then leave the citrus in place while it cooks. However, since citrus would've been extremely expensive in the sort of rural English village that inspired the Shire, they would've saved lemons for recipes where they played a starring role. (If you're not a stickler for period accuracy, feel free to cut a lemon in half, spike it with a couple of cloves, and rub that around the interior as well.)

Gently bruise your rosemary sprigs and stuff them in the cavity along with the two halves of the garlic. Tie the legs together to keep the stuffing in place.

Use your fingers to loosen the skin. Gently slide a tbsp of herb butter under as much skin as possible. Rub another two tbsps of herb butter over the entire bird. Try to coat it as thoroughly as possible. Dot the vegetables with the remaining butter.

Snuggle the bird into its vegetable nest. Roast it at 475F / 245C for 25 minutes. Use a slotted spoon to carefully turn the vegetables surrounding the bird. You want to make sure all of them get a little bit of butter and/or drippings. Return the bird to the oven and continue roasting at 400F / 205C for another 45 minutes or until a meat thermometer plunged into the thickest part of the thigh registers 160F / 162C internal temperature.

Check on the bird around the 30-minute mark. If the skin is getting too crispy, tent some aluminum foil on top to keep it from burning.

When you pull your chicken out of the oven, let it rest for 20 minutes before carving. While it's resting, give the vegetables a good stir to ensure they're coated in butter and drippings. If they're cooked through, turn off the oven and leave them inside it to keep warm. If they're still a little raw in the middle, keep cooking for another 10-15 minutes at 400F / 205C while the chicken rests.

## Easy Chicken Broth for Busy Hobbits

*1 leftover roast chicken carcass*
*2 onions, skin on, quartered*
*2 carrots, broken into pieces*
*2 celery sticks, broken or cut into pieces*
*1 sprig/ 1 tbsp rosemary, thyme or other garden herbs*
*4 garlic cloves, crushed*

After dinner is over, make sure to save the bones, carcass, and any leftover bits. Throw them in a large stockpot. Quarter two whole onions, skin on (the skin adds a delicious caramel color), and throw them in the pot. Add two whole carrots, broken into pieces, and two celery ribs, cut into thirds. If you have any more garden herbs or garlic, throw them in there, too.

Fill the pot with water until ¾ full. Don't worry about an exact amount. This is a ridiculously flexible recipe. Just use your biggest pot. You'll end up with however much broth that pot can contain.

Bring the mess of bones and veggies to a rolling boil. Cover the pot, reduce the heat to medium-low, and let it continue simmering away for at least 2 hours, longer if you have time. Those leftover scraps will miraculously transform into the best darn broth you've ever tasted.

Once you've boiled all the flavor out of the bones, strain out the solids and throw them away. You'll be left with a dark, golden brown chicken broth perfect for use in tomorrow's soup. This makes the perfect base for a nice Mushroom Soup (pg. 66) at Luncheon or an excellent addition to some Savory Mushroom Bread Pudding (pg. 116).

# Savory Bread Pudding with Mushrooms

Savory bread puddings are a great way to transform scraps into a hearty side dish. Like a good Victorian cook, you're using up leftover bread from the previous night's meal and leftover broth from last night's chicken. Add in a few garden herbs and vegetables plus a Hobbit sized helping of mushrooms and suddenly your scraps are the star of your plate.

With a few minor substitutions, this also happens to make a hearty main course for serving any vegans visiting the Shire.

*1 lb / 450 g old, stale bread, cut into cubes*
*3 c / 710 ml chicken stock (pg. 114) or vegetable broth (for vegans)*
*½ c / 115 g butter (or vegetable oil for vegans)*
*8 cloves garlic, minced*
*4 shallots, diced*
*2 onions, diced*
*1 lb / 450 g mixed mushrooms, cleaned and coarsely chopped*
*2 tbsp fresh rosemary*
*1 tbsp rubbed sage*
*½ tbsp fresh thyme*
*1 tsp salt*
*2 large eggs, lightly beaten (omit if vegan)*

To get started, melt 1 tbsp of butter in a large skillet over medium-high heat. Add the chopped onions and shallots. Cook until the onions barely start to brown.

Add the minced garlic, rosemary, sage, thyme, and salt. Keep cooking for 2-3 more minutes, or until the garlic barely starts to brown. Now add the rest of the butter. Let it melt until you vegetables are completely drowned.

Turn off the heat, but leave the skillet in place. Add your 3 cups of broth. This should warm the broth up without bringing it to a boil. Mix the veggies into the broth until you have a thick, soupy blend.

Pour the broth mix over your bread cubes. If you don't have a bowl big enough to handle an entire loaf of bread cut into cubes, divide everything in half and use two bowls. Top the damp bread with your coarsely chopped mushrooms. Use whatever favorites grow in your corner of the Shire.

Finally, add the beaten eggs on top.

Now it's time to get dirty. Roll up your sleeves and use your hands to knead everything together. You want to get some of that flavorful broth and veggies onto every scrap of plain, stale bread while also mixing the mushrooms in as thoroughly as possible. The mix may seem a little dry. Resist the urge to drown it in more broth, or you'll end up with a soggy side dish.

Liberally butter a 9x13 cake pan. Press the mushroom mix into the pan. If you like a dense, heavy bread pudding, keep pressing until there's no air left. If you prefer yours fluffier, more like American Thanksgiving dressing, just pile it in and spread it around.

Either way, bake it uncovered at 350F / 180C for 45 minutes. The top will become a wonderful crunchy brown while the middle stays moist.

If you opted for the loose pile, gently fluff it with a fork before serving. Otherwise, cut it into squares.

**VEGAN VARIATION**

Substitute vegetable broth for chicken broth and the cooking oil of your choice for the butter. If you're using store bought broth, consider doubling the herbs for added flavor. The mix won't stick together well without the eggs, which means you're not going to get neatly cut squares which hold together when being moved from the pan to a plate. Therefore, opt for the fluffy version.

# Wine Braised Oxtails

A lot of people shy away from cuts of meat full of bone and fat. It's a shame because that's where the best flavor hides. In Tolkien's day, nose to tail eating was the norm. A nice segmented oxtail was a great way to get a few bites of rich meat for the whole family with the added bonus of creating a pot of incredibly flavorful broth that would last the week.

*3 lbs / 1.3 kg oxtails*
*1 tbsp butter*
*2 c / 475 ml red wine*
*2 c / 475 ml beef or vegetable broth (whatever you have)*
*2 bay leaves*
*2 sprigs fresh rosemary (about ½ tbsp pulled off the stem)*
*1 whole onion, peeled*
*6 garlic cloves, peeled and crushed*

Melt 1 tbsp butter in a Dutch oven or large, sturdy stockpot. Over medium-high heat, brown the oxtails on all sides. Make sure to brown the fatty side. That adds a lot of flavors.

Once your oxtails are browned up, drown them in red wine and broth. Add the bay leaves, fresh rosemary, crushed garlic cloves, and whole, peeled onion. You can tuck them in a cheesecloth sachet if you'd like to keep things tidy, but it's not strictly necessary.

When the wine and broth mix comes to a boil, put the lid on your Dutch oven. Reduce the heat to low and let it continue simmering for the next 2 hours. Check on the oxtails every half an hour or so to baste them with the cooking liquid.

If you want to make a stew of it, after two hours of cooking, add 3 lbs / 1.3 kg peeled carrots, potatoes, turnips, or the root veggies of your choice. Make sure they're all cut into equal sized pieces no more than 2 inches / 5 cm. Bring the pot back to a boil, then turn the heat down to low and keep simmering for the next 30-45 minutes, or until the veggies are all soft, but not yet falling apart.

If you don't want to make a stew of it, just simmer the oxtails for 2 hours and 45 minutes, or until they're so tender the meat nearly falls off the bone.

Now you have a couple choices. If you're feeling extra rustic, you can serve the oxtails whole and let people pick at them to find all the good bits. However, if you have guests who are a little squeamish about seeing an actual piece of bone on their plate, go ahead and pull the meat off the bone for them. If you're making a stew, pile the meat on top of the vegetables right before serving. If you're just making oxtails, try serving the meat on top of a fresh slice of Boxty (pg. 123).

Before serving, remove 1 cup of fluid from the pot to use as a sauce. You can make an easy gravy by whisking together 2 tbsp flour with ⅓ c cold water until the mix is free of lumps. (If you're allergic to gluten, substitute 1 tsp cornstarch.) Mix the cup of reserved juices into the cold flour water, whisking violently to keep it lump-free. Add salt, pepper, and Worcestershire sauce to spruce it back up.

After dinner (or after picking the bones clean for squeamish guests) return the bones and other leftover bits of the oxtails to the pot. Fill it the rest of the way up with water and bring it back to a boil. You can add a couple carrots and celery sticks for added flavor if you'd like. Let it boil while you entertain your guests at dinner, or for at least 2-3 hours. That gives it time to leach all the last flavor from the bones and marrow. If the night runs late, you can always put everything in a crockpot set to low and forget about it while you go to sleep.

Either way, you now have delicious homemade beef broth you can use in anything. Take a sip, and you'll never want to use store bought broth again. Strain out the solids and store it in the fridge for up to a week.

If you're not in the mood to make broth from the leftovers, at least make sure to strain all the juices out of the pan left after making your gravy. You can make a simple, filling soup of it the next day by adding 1 part water to 1 part juices or just sop it up with stale bread for a truly lazy yet decadent snack.

## Roasted Green Beans

You can't make a meal of meats and carbs alone. Well, you can, actually, but it's nice to have a little something green on the plate, too. When you remove your roast or chicken from the oven, put this side dish in its place. You'll have an easy, no fuss vegetable ready in the time it takes to cool your meat properly.

*1 lb / 450 g fresh green beans, trimmed*
*3 tbsp melted butter*
*2 tbsp fresh basil leaves, sliced thin and bruised*
*1 tsp coarse salt*

Turn your oven down to 400F / 205C.

Spread the butter, basil leaves, and salt over the bottom of a cake pan or baking sheet. Arrange the trimmed green beans on top.

Let the green beans cook for 6 minutes. Stir the pan to evenly distribute the sauce, shake it, so the beans sort themselves back into an even layer, and close the door for another 6-8 minutes. You'll end up with perfectly crisp-tender green beans in a subtly flavored butter sauce.

If you prefer your green beans a little mushier and you have ample space in your oven, you can put them in there along with your chicken and roast for up to half an hour in order to thoroughly soften them up.

**VEGAN VARIATION**

Substitute olive oil for the melted butter. Double the bay leaves and add another ½ tsp of salt to enhance the flavor.

# Beef Braised Carrots

Meat was expensive enough during Tolkien's childhood that few rural families could afford it daily. However, there are lots of tasty ways to stretch out the flavor of meat in an otherwise vegetarian meal. In this case, leftover beef broth brings plenty of taste plus some extra calories and minerals to an inexpensive bunch of carrots.

*2 ¼ lbs / 1 kg carrots, peeled*
*2 c / 475 ml beef broth (or leftover oxtail broth)*
*2 garlic cloves, crushed*
*2 sprigs fresh kitchen herbs (rosemary or thyme)*
*2 tbsp butter*

Sort your carrots to find the ones that are no more than 1 inch / 2.5 cm wide and 6 inches / 15 cm long. Alternately, you could simply cut your carrots into evenly sized pieces, but sometimes it's fun to be a presentation snob. Peel the carrots and cut off any woody end pieces.

Melt the butter in a wide bottomed stock pot. Add the beef broth, crushed garlic cloves, and fresh kitchen herbs. Give it all a good stir and bring the broth to a boil.

Now add your carrots in a single layer and roll them around in the broth a bit. Turn the heat down to medium and let them simmer for 12-15 minutes, or until the carrots are fork-tender. Gently turn them every five minutes to make sure the carrots stay evenly coated.

Once the carrots are nice and tender, remove them with a slotted spoon. Try to keep them intact for presentation purposes.

Turn the heat back up on the broth. Keep boiling until it's reduced to a glaze. Fish out the cloves and any whole herbs then pour the glaze on top of the carrots. In addition to glazing the carrots, this makes a great substitute gravy to help flavor your bread or potatoes.

You can continue the theme of stretching out inexpensive leftovers by serving these carrots with mushroom dressing, mushroom soup, leftover tater cakes from lunch and some leftover roast apple bread for pudding.

**VEGAN VARIATION**

You can use the exact same technique with homemade vegetable broth and a bit of olive oil. It results in a radically different but equally tasty flavor. Try to use homemade veggie broth since the quality of the broth is the real star. The carrots are just there to give it substance and sweetness.

# Boxty on the Griddle

It's no surprise potatoes are one of the only three new world crops Tolkien couldn't bear to ban from the Shire. (He also let them keep coffee and tobacco.) Sure, parsnips and turnips were more nutritious English root vegetables, but nothing can replace the cheap versatility of the simple potato.

Boxty was a thick, family sized potato cake cooked in bacon grease and topped with the cooked bacon. Depending on what else you were doing in your kitchen, it could either be fried on a griddle or baked in a pan. The griddled version makes for a lovely, decadent presentation. You can slice it into quarters as a thrifty main dish or cut it into thinner slices to serve a crowd. Either way, it's one more reason to be grateful Tolkien made an exception to his strict rules about what was eaten in the Shire.

*1 lb / 450 g bacon*
*2 c / 500g potatoes, peeled and grated*
*2 c / 500g mashed potatoes*
*1 ½ c / 225g flour*
*1 tbsp coarse salt*
*1 tsp freshly ground black pepper*
*1 tsp baking powder*
*1 ¼ c / 300ml whole milk*
*¼ c / 55g melted butter*
*2 tbsp butter (for frying)*

Grab your largest skillet and fry up an entire pound of bacon until crispy. This should leave you with a pan full of delicious juices. Set the bacon aside.

While the bacon is frying, peel and grate the raw potatoes until you have 2 cups of shreds. Soak them in cold water for five minutes to wash away the excess starch. Drain the potatoes then refresh them in more cold water.

Mix your flour, salt, pepper, and baking powder in a large bowl. Once those are well blended, add your mashed potatoes, whole milk, and melted butter. Keep mixing until you have a thick, pancake-like batter. Strain the shredded potatoes and add them to the party, mixing just enough to distribute them in the batter evenly.

The next part requires patience. To make one large, family style boxty, you need slow, low, steady heat. Leave your bacon grease filled skillet at a steady medium, no hotter. Pour the batter in and spread it around the skillet until you have a single, giant pancake, no more than ½ inch / 1.25 cm thick. If you have any leftover batter, get out a second skillet and make some baby boxty's fried in butter.

Let the bix boxty cook for about ten minutes. You can use a spatula to peek under the edge in order to make sure it isn't burning, but do your best to just leave it in peace. Once the underside is a nice, golden brown, carefully slide it out onto a plate.

Add the last 2 tbsp of butter to the pan and let it melt. Now carefully, quickly, put the buttered pan on top of your plate and flip it over, so the raw batter side goes splat down onto the hot skillet.

Put the boxty back on the medium heat and let it continue cooking for another 10 minutes, or until golden brown on both sides.

Slide your glorious disc of boxty onto a large plate. Remember all that bacon you fried? Tear it into small pieces and pile them on top of the boxty. If you're making oxtails for people who are averse to seeing bones on a plate, you can also pull all the meat off the oxtails and pile it on top of the boxty then serve it with oxtail gravy on the side.

**VEGAN VARIATION**

Purists will say you can't have a proper boxty without bacon. However, in lean times families might cut the bacon in half or even down to a quarter the usual quantity. Think of the vegan variation as being extra thrifty.

Substitute 2 tbsp of your favorite vegan cooking oil for the bacon grease and an equal quantity of oil for the butter. You can also substitute in your favorite non-dairy substitute for the whole milk, but try to get one that actually has some fat. To enhance the flavor, add 1 heaping tsp each of onion powder, garlic powder, and black pepper into the flour mix. You don't want to add any herbs because the long cooking time and griddle method could cause any in the crust to burn.

# Yorkshire pudding

Purists say you can't have a real Yorkshire pudding without beef drippings from a prime rib roast. There's no arguing that the drippings give this classic English side a distinctive flavor, but you can still make a pretty darn tasty Yorkshire pudding using pretty much any flavorful fat you like.

*3 large eggs, at room temperature*
*1 1/2 c / 355 ml milk, at room temperature*
*3/4 tsp table salt*
*1 1/2 c / 200 g flour*
*3 tbsp beef drippings or the fat of your choice*

Yorkshire Puddings are actually made from a handful of simple, everyday ingredients. In fact, other than the beef drippings, the only thing separating a Yorkshire pudding from a pancake is technique.

Mix the milk, eggs, and salt until smooth and creamy. Add the flour and keep mixing until the batter is completely smooth and free of lumps. Pour it into a pitcher and let it rest for at least half an hour.

For best results, you want to make the batter in advance then let it sit for a good while before baking. Thirty minutes is the minimum, but feel free to mix up the batter in the morning and let it sit all day while you're at work.

When you're ready to make your Yorkshire Puddings, start by heating your oven to 450F / 230C. Grab a sturdy metal muffin pan and add 1 tsp of beef drippings, butter, lard, or the fat of your choice to each well. Put the pan in the oven and leave it there for 4-5 minutes, or until the fat is completely melted.

When your pan is scorching hot, very quickly pull it out and, as fast as you can, fill each well ⅓ high with batter. As soon as you fill the last well, put the pan right back in the oven and close the door.

Now for the hard part. Do not open the oven door for the next 20 minutes. If you do, your puddings may collapse. Leave them alone and let them rise into gloriously crispy domes with a hollow interior begging to be filled with gravy.

## VEGAN VARIATION

Purists will balk, but you can make a shockingly acceptable vegan Yorkshire pudding using almond or soy milk instead of dairy and the fat of your choice instead of beef drippings. Consider adding ½ tsp garlic powder to the batter for an extra savory element.

# Chester Pudding

Chester Pudding is an eggier, almond infused, Victorian ancestor of the modern Lemon Meringue Pie. One of the nice things about this historic dessert is the kinder, gentler meringue standing a mere two inches / 2.5 cm high. Instead of stressing over creating the airiest of egg whites, relax and enjoy the simple wholesomeness of a moderately fancy looking pie that has a mere seven ingredients.

**Crust:**
*1 ½ c / 200 g flour*
*¾ c / 100 g butter, softened*
*¼ c /50 g sugar*
*1 tbsp water*

**Filling:**
*6 eggs, yolks, and whites separated*
*⅓ c / 70 g sugar*
*zest of 1 medium lemon*
*juice of 1 medium lemon*
*¾ c /100 g butter, softened*
*½ c /50 g almond flour*

Start by making the pastry crust. Mix the flour and sugar. Now add the softened butter and work in into the mix until it becomes crumbly little pebbles. Add the water, a little at a time, until the dough is just barely sticky enough to hold together. When in doubt, err on the side of less water rather than more.

Once the crumbly mix is transformed into a dense dough, gently knead it a couple of times then put it in the fridge for at least 15 minutes.

When the dough has cooled down, roll it out, so it'll fit into an 8 inch / 20 cm tart pan. Press the dough into the pan, making sure it extends up the sides, and trim off any remainder on top. Feel free to turn the spare dough into Plum Heavies for tomorrow's Afternoon Tea.

To make the filling, first, separate the egg yolks from the egg whites. The two have very different roles to play in this pie.

Add the sugar, lemon juice, lemon zest, and softened butter to the egg yolks and whisk them together until the mix is completely smooth. This will be the base of the pie filling.

If you have a double boiler, add the eggy mix to the top and a few inches of water to the bottom. Bring the water to a gentle boil and continually whisk the lemon mix for 3-4 minutes until it thickens to the consistency of custard. If you don't have a double boiler, you can always put an oven safe glass bowl on top of a regular pot. Fill the pot with a few inches of water, but not enough to touch the bottom of the bowl. You'll achieve the same effect as a double boiler without any special equipment. Just be extra careful handling the bowl, as it will be dangerously hot.

Pour the filling into the pie crust and bake for 20-25 min at 400F / 205C.

While the pie filling bakes, prepare the meringue. Victorians would have whisked this by hand until their arms were sore ("until a maid is completely worn," is a common instruction in period cookbooks) but you're welcome to use a hand mixer or stand mixer. Beat the whites for about 3 minutes, then add half the almonds. Keep beating for another 1-2 minutes, or until the meringue is barely starting to firm up, then add the rest of the almonds. Continue beating until the egg whites are light and fluffy. Don't keep going past that point, though, or you risk them collapsing.

When 25 minutes are up, pull the pie out of the oven and quickly spread the meringue on top. Stretch it out in an even layer from edge to edge. Pop the pie back in the oven for another 10-15 minutes, or until the meringue stiffens up and the top turns a light golden brown.

Let the pie cool for 10-15 minutes before serving, but not much longer. It's best served while still warm and slightly runny in the middle.

# Roasted Apples

Roasted Apples are a great period dessert on their own, but they're even better as leftovers. You can use them as an ingredient in bread for tomorrow's Elevenses, diced up to top tomorrow's oatmeal porridge, or even as a sauce for a nice pork chop. Don't be afraid to double the recipe, so you'll have some to eat tonight and more to use tomorrow.

*4 large, tart apples*
*1 c / 235 ml sweet white wine*
*8 tbsp butter*
*¼ c / 50 g sugar*
*4 tbsp cinnamon*
*2 tbsp ginger*
*1 tbsp nutmeg*
*½ tbsp allspice*
*¼ tbsp cloves*
*1 c / 220 g currants or minced raisins*
*½ c / 110 g chopped almonds or walnuts (optional)*

Gently wash any wax or residue off your apples.

Use a spoon to core the apples. Don't use an apple corer. You want to dig most of the way down while making sure to keep the bottom intact.

Arrange the apples in a square baking dish. If you can, you want them to be as snug as possible to help keep them from losing shape. Pour the white wine on top.

While the apples relax in their wine bath, mix 4 tbsp room temperature butter with the sugar, cinnamon, ginger, nutmeg, allspice, and cloves. Once the butter and spices are a well-blended mix in the currants (or minced raisins) and nuts if you're using them.

Stuff each apple with ¼ of the mix.

Top each well of stuffing with another 1 tbsp of butter.

Bake at 375F / 190C for 35-40 minutes, or until the apples are tender but not mushy. Baste the apples twice during baking. As soon as you take them out of the oven, baste them with the baking liquid again.

If you have more leftovers than you can reasonably use in the next day or two, chop up the apples, mix them with the remaining sauce, and freeze individual portions.

## VEGAN VARIATION

Use 4 tbsp coconut oil in place of the 8 tbsp of butter. Yes, that's less fat, but excess coconut oil makes these taste oddly greasy. Add ½ tsp of salt along with the spices.

# Appendix

## VEGAN

Apple and Cherry Griddle Cakes - pg. 23
Apple Hand Pies Two Ways - pg. 34
Bannocks - pg. 89
Braised Carrots - pg. 121
Boxy on the Griddle - pg. 125
Carrot Cake - pg. 78
Ginger Oat Bread - pg. 47
Mushroom and Bacon Hash - pg. 12
Mushroom Soup - pg. 69
Pan Fried Tater Cakes - pg. 71
Porter Cake - pg. 39
Roasted Apples - pg. 131
Roasted Asparagus - pg. 97
Roasted Green Beans - pg. 120
Rosemary Skillet Peas - pg. 101
Rustic Apple Tart - pg. 106
Savory Bread Pudding with Mushrooms - pg. 116
Small Adventure Sized Mincemeat Pies - pg. 51
Stewed Apples and Prunes - pg. 17
Stuffed Roasted Mushrooms - pg. 103
Yorkshire pudding - pg. 123

## VEGETARIAN
### All Vegan Recipes plus the following:

Braided Mushroom and Cheese Bread - pg. 54
Chelsea Buns - pg. 57
Chester Pudding - pg. 128
Country Gingersnaps - pg. 87
Furmity - pg. 19
Honey Cakes - pg. 43
Hot Buttered Shire Scones - pg. 83
Hot Cross Buns - pg. 91
Lemon and Lavender Bread - pg. 109
Morning Oat Porridge - pg. 18
Mushroom Omelet - pg. 26
Plum Heavies - pg. 81
Roasted Apple Bread - pg. 49
Stuffed Poached Pears - pg. 21
Seed Cakes - pg. 45
Shortbread - pg. 85
Short Crust Pastry Dough - pg. 29
Steak and Ale Pie - pg. 63
Strawberries and Cream Bread - pg. 75

## GLUTEN FREE

Braised Carrots – pg. 121
Country Sausage – pg. 15
Morning Oat Porridge - pg. 18
Mushroom and Bacon Hash - pg. 12
Mushroom Omelet - pg. 26
Mushroom Soup - pg. 69
Rack of Lamb - pg. 95
Roasted Asparagus - pg. 97
Roast Chicken - pg. 113
Roast Chicken Broth - pg. 114
Roasted Green Beans - pg. 120
Roasted Lamb Broth - pg. 96
Rosemary Skillet Peas - pg. 101
Scotch Eggs - pg. 61
Steak and Ale Pie - pg. 63
Stewed Apples and Prunes - pg. 17
Stuffed Poached Pears - pg. 21
Wine Braised Oxtails - pg. 119

## PALEO/PRIMAL

Braised Carrots - pg. 121
Country Sausage - pg. 15
Lemon and Pepper Baked Fish - pg. 73
Mushroom Omelet - pg. 26
Mushroom Soup - pg. 69
Rack of Lamb - pg. 95
Roasted Asparagus - pg. 97
Roast Chicken - pg. 113
Roast Chicken Broth - pg. 114
Roasted Lamb Broth - pg. 96
Stewed Apples and Prunes - pg. 17
Wine Braised Oxtails - pg. 119

# Eye of Sauron

Hobbitses can not take my precious. The Eye will stop them. Fill their bellies, it will! Then, when they cannot move, they will be mine, all mine!

**1 tube crescent dough**

**8 large pasta shells**

**8 premade meatballs**

**1 cup red pasta sauce**

**8 tsp shredded mozzarella**

Boil their ~~shells~~ eyes till soft and tender.

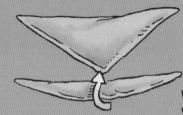

Unroll the crescent dough, all pale and weak, weaker than Smeagol it is, and roll it up like eyeless worms in a dark cave..

The worms are for you. Yes, U! Make them into a U! So pale, so weak. Must bake for 10-12 minutes until golden as my precious.

Heat your sauce until it's as warm as blood and heat your meatballs till they're as warm and trembly as hobbitses knees.

Each eye is filled with one bloody tablespoon of sauce. Each bleeding socket plugged with one tasty meatball.

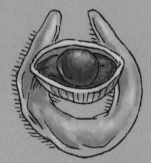

Now, you must place Sauron's all seeing eye into its crescent socket.

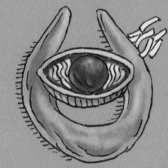

Sprinkle the edges of his eye with cheeses all milky and white like the tears of elveses.

Wash it down with salty blood and crunchy bones and sweet lemon donuts, almost as sweet as my precious.

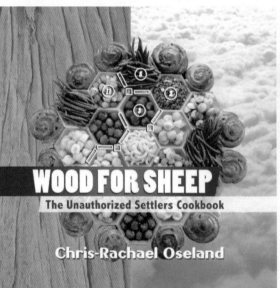

Visit Kitchen Overlord for hundreds of geektastic recipes representing all your favorite fandoms.

Printed in Great Britain
by Amazon